NARROW ROAD TO HEAVEN

Prayers & Scriptures

DARREN PETTIS

Copyright © 2021 Darren Pettis.

All rights reserved. No part of this book may be used or reproduced by any means, graphic, electronic, or mechanical, including photocopying, recording, taping or by any information storage retrieval system without the written permission of the author except in the case of brief quotations embodied in critical articles and reviews.

WestBow Press books may be ordered through booksellers or by contacting:

WestBow Press
A Division of Thomas Nelson & Zondervan
1663 Liberty Drive
Bloomington, IN 47403
www.westbowpress.com
844-714-3454

Because of the dynamic nature of the Internet, any web addresses or links contained in this book may have changed since publication and may no longer be valid. The views expressed in this work are solely those of the author and do not necessarily reflect the views of the publisher, and the publisher hereby disclaims any responsibility for them.

Any people depicted in stock imagery provided by Getty Images are models, and such images are being used for illustrative purposes only. Certain stock imagery © Getty Images.

Unless marked otherwise, all Scripture quotations are taken from the New King James Version®. Copyright © 1982 by Thomas Nelson. Used by permission. All rights reserved.

Scripture quotations marked NIV are taken from The Holy Bible, New International Version®, NIV® Copyright © 1973, 1978, 1984, 2011 by Biblica, Inc.® Used by permission. All rights reserved worldwide.

ISBN: 978-1-6642-3277-8 (sc)
ISBN: 978-1-6642-3278-5 (hc)
ISBN: 978-1-6642-3276-1 (e)

Library of Congress Control Number: 2021910587

Print information available on the last page.

WestBow Press rev. date: 5/22/2021

CONTENTS

Acknowledgements vii
Foreword... ix
Introduction xi

Chapter 1   Praying to God.. 1
Chapter 2   Answered Prayers 21
Chapter 3   When God Speaks 47
Chapter 4   He Never Let's Go 67
Chapter 5   Saved through Faith... 83
Chapter 6   Wherever God Leads 101
Chapter 7   Rain, Fear, and Fire...115
Chapter 8   Be Still 129
Chapter 9   Short Prayers 139
Chapter 10 Our Heavenly Father 163
Chapter 11 The Word of God 173
Chapter 12 Spirit of Power.. 187

Bibliography... 205
About the Author... 207

ACKNOWLEDGEMENTS

First and foremost, I am eternally grateful to God for blessing me with the chance to share His word. Through His grace and mercies upon me, I have more than I deserve in this life through the people He has placed around me. I therefore need to thank them in no particular order. I am also indebted to my beautiful and lovely wife, Becky, for putting up with me in the course of the past years. Thank you for your love and support. A big kudos and deep gratitude goes to our beautiful daughters, Caitlin, Lindsey, and Cameron for their input in the process of writing this book. A special thanks to my lovely Mom, my brother, Mike, and His wife, Dana, and their children, Hunter, and Holli, and our lovely grandchildren, Kennedy, Harrison, and Lennox.

FOREWORD

If we're charting a new course, it often helps to walk with someone who already knows the way. If you want to enhance your prayer life, walk alongside Darren Pettis in his *Narrow Road to Heaven*. This book will encourage you to pray, and you'll be blessed to listen in on many of Darren's own biblically-based prayers.

Mark Hudgins | Membership Pastor

Ingleside Baptist Church
834 Wimbish Road
Macon, Georgia 31210
478.477.7251 | www.ingleside.org

INTRODUCTION

Someone once asked me, "Why Narrow Road to Heaven?". It's not only the title of this book; it's also the name we gave to our global ministry. In Matthew 7:13-14, Jesus told us that there is a broad gate that many follow, which leads to destruction and death, and there is a narrow gate few follow but leads to life. We are therefore obliged to take the narrow path, which leads to heaven and everlasting life.

Jesus commanded us to spread the gospel all over the world. This is the reason we started Narrow Road to Heaven which now has over seventy thousand followers. Our outreach through the ministry spans the world from The Philippines, to Japan, India, Africa, Saudi Arabi, Iraq, Afghanistan.

One day on a whim, I began to write prayers primarily for Christians but also for non-Christians. In 2012, I opened a page on social media called Narrow Road to Heaven offering daily scriptures as God's Word for the day. After receiving a tremendous response from visitors to that page, I realized that people wanted to read prayers and make them their own. Not only did they want them, but also, they also *needed* them.

People would request prayers for their spouses, or sick relatives and needs for their friends and loved ones so frequently that I started to post one or two prayers a week. As the fan base grew, these prayers were reaching two million people every week. I was astounded but more so encouraged to realize that God would use me as His tool to inspire and guide people on how to pray—and up to now, I am simply amazed at how He uses me to spread the Good News of the Gospel of Jesus Christ.

The idea of a book never crossed my mind until the day my wife suggested it. I did not think anything of it then. The thought kept coming back to me, though. *"I am not writing a book,"*—I said to myself, *"—I am posting prayers and scriptures on my social media page."* Weeks later, my wife mentioned it again. This time I took it to God in prayer and from that moment, God placed it in my heart to start a book on prayer.

My favorite book to read in the Holy Bible is Psalms. In it, King David had poured his heart out to God. Reading psalms helped me better understand not only God's ways but, more importantly, how to communicate with Him. Words such as *leading me, guiding me, directing me, or showing me your good ways* come to us from David's prayers to God, which I have incorporated in my own way into the prayers I have written in this book.

I grew up attempting to read the King James Version, which can be challenging to follow for a young child. Though I still quote verses in my mind from that version, I read from the New King James Version (NJKV) now. It is more modern and somewhat easily understood. I do not knock other translations. The NJKV is what I am accustomed to reading. So, unless noted, I quote from it throughout the book.

Narrow Road to Heaven: Prayers & Scriptures is a project guided by our Heavenly Father and through the Holy Spirit. Before writing a prayer, I asked God for His inspiration and guidance. Each prayer is set up in a certain way. The method is very much like how Jesus taught us how to pray to the Father in the Lord's Prayer. Most prayers follow a certain pattern, first by praising God, asking for our needs, asking for forgiveness, asking for protection, and then praising God once more. Naturally, all prayers have an ending phrase. God told us to us ask for anything in His Son's name. Therefore, all prayers end in Jesus's name with an Amen, suggesting, "So be it."

Some chapters have prayers followed by relevant scriptures. Other chapters discuss times when God is silent, when we go through difficult times, how to pray to Him, how to listen to God, and wherever He leads. The specific chapters are a combination of prayers and scriptures intertwined with biblical explanations and explain how God interacts with us.

Figuring out how to pray to our Heavenly Father needs to be treated like a learning process. We are not born spiritually linked to God. Instead, we were born into sin and so must learn the correct way to pray to God. Additionally, a spiritual line to God requires a mediator. One who would open the ears of God, and Jesus is that mediator. He makes us righteous with God, thereby making our prayers heard.

God placed it in my heart that I was going to be a significant factor in the gospel of Jesus Christ. At first, I attempted to become a medical doctor, but that was not my path. God had other plans for me. I followed God's plan that He designed for me. I understood what He meant for me. God taught me to love others, and everything else would fall into place. He taught me that if I had love, then I was from Him. Every day is truly a blessing from God because I want to bless others, as is His will. It took years for me to figure that out. Now, I am who I am, and it's by the grace of God.

Narrow Road to Heaven: Prayers & Scriptures seeks to enlighten and inspire readers on how spiritually connected we can be to God through prayer. I strive to please our Lord as well as to be pleasing to the reader. I hope that He blesses you abundantly while reading this book that God inspires you to share the message in it to enlighten others. Spread the good news of the gospel of Jesus Christ, our Lord, and savior.

Pray like a warrior.
Darren Pettis
Macon, Georgia
February 2021

Narrow Road to Heaven: *Prayers & Scriptures*

Enter by the narrow gate; for wide is the gate and broad is the way that leads to destruction, and there are many who go in by it. Because narrow is the gate and difficult is the way which leads to life, and there are few who find it—Matthew 7:13–14

*God doesn't move in your life when you struggle.
He moves when you pray.*—Charles Stanley

CHAPTER 1
Praying to God

"Then you will call upon Me and go and pray to Me, and I will listen to you. And you will seek Me and find Me, when you search for Me with all your heart"—Jeremiah 29:12–13

Praying to God

I do not think anyone on earth can be labeled an expert on how to pray to God. A prayer from a child may take the cake. Hearing a child pray is one of the most precious moments to witness. Children learn to pray simple prayers such as, *"God is great, God is good. Let us thank Him for our food. By His hands we are fed, give us Lord our daily bread. Amen"*.

My mom prayed with me every night at bedtime, *"Now I lay me down to sleep. I pray the Lord, my soul to keep. If I die before I wake, I pray the Lord, my soul, to take"*. I prayed with my children at bedtime, *"Now I lay me down to sleep. I pray the Lord, my soul, to keep. May angels watch me through the night and wake me with the morning light"*. Any prayer such as these travels straight to the ear of God. As we get older, some people may lose the desire to pray because of unanswered prayers—they give up too easily. Some people may have never prayed, simply because they do not know how.

Here is the exciting news. By the end of this book you will have God answering your prayers. You will learn what to say and what to ask for. You'll be a prayer warrior real soon. Wherever you are sitting, close your eyes and bow your head. Reflect on God in heaven for a moment—don't say anything yet—think of Him reaching His hand out to you. Now, grab His hand. There it is—a free, direct line to God in spiritual communication—start praying.

It is a privilege to pray to our Heavenly Father. No one can force us to do it, however, so it should be something that we want to do. Anything that we attempt for the first time can seem a bit awkward. Ever try ice skating and remember the fear of falling onto the hard ice? For most of us, what we feared actually took place. Nevertheless, we got up and tried it again. All new endeavors may seem uncomfortable and strange initially. Once we get the hang of it and continue to perform them, they eventually become second nature.

Praying to our Heavenly Father does not come naturally. Our spiritual linkage to God must be cultivated. We were not born with it. We were born spiritually dead as a result of Adam's sin.

Twenty-five years ago, I was into prayer more than ever. Yet, I did not know how to pray in such a way that God would respond to me. I just asked for things that I wanted. You know, the typical *"Give me this, God"* or *"Let me have success, God"* types of prayers. Praying was something that I was exceptionally good at failing at. I was an expert on how *not* to pray to God. I would pray one exact way to God, and when that prayer did not work, I would pray another way. I read many books on prayer that gave some insight and examples, but even they did not help. I got discouraged at times, but I persisted, knowing God would show me the way. I asked Him about how to pray to Him. I just told Him that I could not figure this prayer thing out, and I needed His help. What I learned, and it is the central theme throughout this book, was how to seek and do the will of God. We learn God's will by asking Him in prayer as well as by reading His Holy Word.

TEACH ME YOUR WILL

Heavenly Father, there is none greater than you. You are an awesome God. I praise your holy name all day long and love you with my whole heart. I come to you on bended knees and with an open heart, seeking your instruction and wisdom.

Father, you remember my past prayers that were of selfish desires. You listened to my supplications, while I went without your divine counsel. I asked of things based on my own will instead of praying that I would do yours. I acknowledge my mistake Lord; please forgive me in Jesus's name. Purge my heart from selfish desires and fill it with the desire to do your will in my life.

Teach me to understand and do your will that you have set for me in my life. Show me your good ways and guide me with your eyes upon me. Direct my steps to walk in righteousness. Open my mouth to speak truthfulness. Let my hands extend with love as the love you have shown me. Be the flame that shines brightly in my heart so that others may see your good works in me.

Father, strengthen my faith to abide by your holy ways always. During the darkest moments, I know you are still with me. You never forsake me. You hold faithful to your promises. You are the light that gets me through the storm, my refuge, my fortress, my shield, and my buckler. No fear shall take away the love you have for me. I trust in you with all my heart, and my understanding is always in you. When I am weak, I gain strength through you.

Grant my family and me financial blessings. But also rain down your sweet grace from your loving heart. Show abundant blessings to those who reverently fear and love you wholeheartedly. Take away from me the burden and worry for the things in my life. Secure me with the warmth of your comforting love, grace, and mercy. Let my eyes see holy things and allow my ears to be deaf to worldly ones.

Father, I acknowledge my iniquities against you. Take my transgressions, through the blood of the lamb, Jesus Christ, my redeemer, and savior. Throw them into the sea of forgetfulness. Wash me with your precious grace, cleaning me white as snow.

Show healing to those who are sick, and heal their bodies with your almighty power. Uplift the spirits of those who are facing difficult times. Bring them near to your heart and show them your tender mercies. I pray for those who have done wrong to me and for those who have hate in their hearts. Lord, open their hearts so they may see the love you give freely. Open the hearts of nonbelievers that they might know you wish no one to perish but live eternally in your kingdom.

Father, I praise and worship your name all day long. Thank you, Father, for giving me your unconditional love. Shield and protect me from evil and deliver me from temptation. Guard my heart with the peace of Christ. Forgive me of my sins.

In Jesus's name, I pray.
Amen.

God's Language

After a long period of praying without success, I felt a tug. It kept pulling me more and more toward His Word. Gradually, I developed a daily practice of reading the Bible. I began to memorize several verses and pray. Before long, I found myself reciting those scriptures in prayer.

Wow! There is such power in the scriptures. My prayers became meaningful, scripturally based prayers. As I began reciting certain verses and adding dialogue when talking to God, they also became effective. That's because of my newfound confidence. And as it grew, I felt more comfortable praying to God—I prayed more. I developed an intimate relationship with Him through my daily practice of just talking in His language—the scripture.

RINGING THE BELLS IN HEAVEN

Dear, Heavenly Father, excellent is your name in all the earth and all its fullness. I worship and praise your holy name and love you wholeheartedly. I lift my arms toward heaven seeking your divine counsel and wisdom.

Father, I ring the bells in heaven so that my voice may reach your ear. Hear my supplications; hear my cry to you, Lord. You tested my heart and kept me from the snare of the fowler and the depths of the sinking pit. You have set me up in a broad place with your eyes upon me.

When I kept my sins to myself, my body ached, and I became restless. But you Lord forgave me when I confessed my transgressions against you. You have washed my sins from my heart with the blood of the lamb. I am now cleansed white as snow. Thank you for your never-ending grace.

Father, I need you every hour of every day. You are my defense; you are my righteousness. I am nothing without you. I rejoice in your righteousness and good ways. You raise me when I am down. You are my light in dark places. You hide me in your secret place and cover me under the shadow of your wings. I shall not fear man nor evil, for you are my strength in times of trouble. I walk with integrity and stand on solid ground; I shall not be moved.

When I get angry, you tell me not to sin. When I am anxious, you ask me to be still. Father, your Word tells me to wait on the Lord and be of good courage, and you will strengthen my heart. My soul waits for you, Lord. I put all my trust in you because you care for me.

Teach me your perfect ways. Guide my heart always to follow your will in my life. Keep me from selfish desires. Clean my heart from anything that is not acceptable to you and fill it with truthfulness and righteousness. Mold me to be more like your beloved Son, Jesus Christ, whom you sent for the salvation of all humanity.

You have clothed my soul with joy and gladness. I may shed a tear at night, but joy comes in the morning. My eyes are forever focused on you. I may fail you, Father, but you never fail me. You are always by my side. You reward me with your loving-kindness and tender mercies. I marvel at the love, grace, and mercy that you have shown to a sinner like me. Who is like you? There is none greater than you Father. You are the Most High and the king of glory.

Father, show favor to my family and me. Rain down abundant blessings on us, Lord. Show them to all who love you with all their heart. Heal the sick with your marvelous healing wonders and lift the broken-hearted. Secure their heart with the warmth of your unconditional love. Father, I forgive those who have done wrong against me just as you have forgiven me. Teach me to love my enemies and those who have hate in their hearts. Let my hand extend loving-kindness to all, as you have shown to me. Let the words of my mouth rejoice in the glory of your salvation.

I praise your holy name in the morning. I praise it all day long. Lift your hand Father and be merciful to me and hear my prayer. Direct my steps through the Holy Spirit to walk in obedience to your will. Guard and comfort my heart with the peace of Christ. Deliver me from temptation and from evil. Forgive me of my sins.

In Jesus's name, I pray.
Amen!

A Prayer of Moses

"I pray, if I have found grace in Your sight, show me now Your way, that I may know You" (Exodus 33:13).

Pray, Pray, and Pray

The apostle Paul tells us to, "Pray without ceasing" (1Thessalonians 5:17). King David prayed seven times a day, while Daniel prayed three times a day, even when it was against the law (Daniel 6:10). Prayer is our primary duty and how we show spiritual devotion to our Heavenly Father.

Praying three or seven times a day seemed to me excessive, even obsessive. What did Paul mean when he wrote "Pray without ceasing?" Praying one time to God may seem to be a struggle, much less seven times a day. If we prayed without ceasing, people would have us locked up in some facility in the middle of nowhere in a padded room receiving pills three to seven times a day. Praying without ceasing can be a challenge.

We have to make time to spend it with God in prayer. If God is in spirit, and we pray in the spirit, we can pray in our mind, anywhere and anytime. For example, while walking to the vending machine at work, you can pray, "Lord, please help my coworker who just lost their husband in a car wreck. Help her take care of and feed her three kids. Please forgive me for my selfishness. And thank you for the protection of my family. Bless my coworker; heal her broken and crushed heart. I pray this in Jesus's name. Amen."

Praying without ceasing means we can pray at any given time or place. Paul is not suggesting we pray continuously. He is saying, just as Jesus told us, that we must be persistent. Keep praying and keep asking God to answer us.

If your prayers have been unanswered, maybe you threw in the towel too early and gave up. The late Zig Ziglar said, "Good things come to those who believe, better things come to those who are patient, and the best things come to those who don't give up." God loves persistence. Bug Him. Call on Him until He answers your prayer. I am confident in saying this because Jesus said it.

Amen.

The Spiritual Doorway

Have you ever walked into a room to pick up a certain item? However, as soon as you crossed the threshold, you forgot what it was you went to retrieve. It happens to me often. I'm sure it has happened to you too.

Distortion

Professor Gabriel Radvansky from the University of Notre Dame studied this very thing with people of varying IQs. The results were surprising. It turns out that when we go from one room to another, we leave our thoughts behind at the door as we enter a new space. Researchers believe that walking through doors or changing rooms resets our memory. That's to make room for new memories. This strange phenomenon is called the location updating effect or the "doorway" effect[1]. If this ever happens to you, do not worry. It happens to everyone. Our brain works that way!

The point here, friends, is that in prayer, you leave the earthly realm and enter the spiritual realm of God. Since, your thoughts are spiritual, you have opened the "spiritual doorway" to begin your conversation with Him.

Prayer is the "spiritual doorway" to God that enables us to interact with Him. It is like having a personal and relational conversation with God. We become closer to God by pulling on the rope and ringing the bells in heaven.

In an upcoming section, we will review the things that need to be in our prayer. We bring to God our sins, our needs, and our desires to the throne of grace (Hebrews 4:16). When we talk, He listens. When God speaks, we listen. The point here is talking. That is one of the significant aspects of prayer—Talking to God.

Butterflies

You remember that "fluttery" feeling you got every time you were with that certain person. The one whom you were just head over heels about? Your face flushed, heart raced, and your stomach did flips. We have all experienced this sensation. It happens when you feel nervous, anxious, or frightened.

Imagine being on a camping trip and encountering a giant grizzly bear. "Oh, Lord! Where are those butterflies when you need them?" you'd be thinking. Your brain receives the impulses through your central nervous system, saying, "Give me something so I can run extremely fast." So, it sends a signal to the adrenal glands to release a hormone called adrenaline.

This physiological response causes a few things to happen. It increases your heart rate to pump blood faster, in this case, to your legs. It elevates your breathing rate to allow more oxygen to the muscles. It causes your pupils to dilate so you can see more effectively while running through the woods; The release of adrenaline is a naturally occurring part of the "fight or flight" response. I can assume most people would pick the flight response in this scenario—"Run Forest, run!"

Sometimes in awkward moments, such as when speaking in front of crowds, we want to run away or ball up in a corner and hide. Our stomach gets this weird sensation, and our palms become sweaty. Our heart begins pumping over one hundred beats per minute. This physiological response is normal. Blood is leaving your stomach and going to your heart, brain, and muscles. That's what is causing that fluttery butterfly feeling in your stomach.

What's more, feeling that way is a common thing for people involved in different endeavors. I saw an interview on T.V. a while back. A famous actor was saying, "The day I don't have butterflies is the day I will quit acting."

In the same vein, praying in front of a group of people may make you feel uncomfortable. The thing is, praying to God should be anxiety free. He is not going to judge you. He knows how nervous you may be. So, welcome the butterflies and pray from your heart.

Spill the Beans

Some people have mentioned they do not know what to say when praying, which causes them anxiety. Or you're simply exhausted by the end of the day, and your brain goes blank. Your mind may become discombobulated as you search for the right words to say. However, the Holy Spirit intercedes and relays your prayer to God from your heart—true prayer comes from the heart.

While we may keep certain secrets close to our hearts in our daily lives, God wants us to spill them to Him. He already knows what is in our hearts. He wants us to voice it to Him. In a way, praying to God is simply telling Him what is on our minds or what is troubling our hearts. When I did not know what to say, I brought up God's promises, such as, "Father, your Word says you will never leave me or forsake me that you will hold me up with your righteous right hand." That is God's promise to you and me. God does not go back on His Word; He is faithful to His promises.

Scripturally based prayers speak His language. Read the following example: "Dear Father, your Word says to be strong and courageous. I have no fear other than a reverent fear of you because you are always on my side. Your Word tells me that you will teach me the way to go with your eyes upon me. Give me wisdom and understanding of your ways. Your Word is proven, and your ways are perfect. You are the fire that warms my heart and the light that directs my steps".

Every individual on this planet is unique, and each has their unique way of praying, In other words, there is no one right way to talk to God. What you find here, too, is simply a method that I have found helpful. If you need to kickstart learning how to pray, it makes for an excellent template. Regardless of what we say or the words we choose for our prayer, God puts them into action. And He causes them to become powerful.

Fly Like an Eagle

The eagle is one of the fiercest raptors in the sky. It has extraordinary vision—it's eight times greater than that of humans. An eagle can sight its prey from up to two miles; that is phenomenal. It can kill its target with its razor, sharp claws, called talons. Other eagles, such as the snake eagle, lift their prey high in the sky, bite off its head and, swallow it whole.

The eagle is the king of the sky. The snake eagle takes his battle to the sky, where he defeats its enemy. We need to raise our prayers to God in the spiritual sky where the enemy is weak and vulnerable. Soar into the spiritual realm of God in heaven, and feed on His Word and righteousness. Take a leap of faith to step out of your comfort zone, and empty your soul honestly and wholeheartedly.

A mother eagle provides for her eaglets for several years. After the eaglet has reached a certain age, she begins to take apart the nest piece by piece. Then begins to nudge the eaglets out of the nest. An eaglet, terrified with fear, screeches and clings to the nest for dear life. The mother eagle continues this process until the eaglet's wings become stronger and stronger. Eventually, the mother nudges it once more, and "whoosh," the eaglet soars from the nest, flaps its wings, and flies boldly into the sky.

Our transformation to step out in faith may require some nudging as well. We resist change and want to cling to what is safe,—what is familiar. If you're stuck in a comfort zone, you can become stagnant—you are not going anywhere. However, when you step out onto the stage of non-comfortability,—your life has just begun anew. Your Christian wings become stronger, enabling you to fly to the heavens spiritually. Reach out, fly boldly with Christ and see how far you soar with Him.

God's word tells us, "But those who wait on the Lord shall renew their strength; They shall mount up with wings like eagles, they shall run and not be weary, they shall walk and not faint" (Isaiah 40:31). You are about to learn the power of prayer and, most of all—, how prayer changes you.

Prayer Privilege

Praying to God is talking to Him. Tell your problems to God and make them His issues. That is how close our Heavenly Father wants us to be to Him. Tell God what is on your mind. Give Him all your worldly problems—all your pain, guilt, and sorrow. Feel it in your soul that God is pulling out those negative things hurting you. At the same time, He is pouring love, peace, and joy into your heart.

You are in a spiritual realm now; let God take control. He wants to bless us more than we can ever dream. Turn it over to the Lord and watch His mighty power start to transform your life. It could be merely asking God for guidance about making a job change. It may be you asking God to send you a godly person whom you want to marry. Whatever you feel like talking to Him about, let God know what has you concerned—and do it from your heart.

HEAVENLY FATHER

Dear Heavenly Father, we come to you with thanksgiving. We worship, praise, and adore you with our whole hearts. We raise our hands toward heaven seeking your mighty good works, your counsel, and divine protection.

Lord, you are the Kings of kings and the Lord of lords. We put all our trust in you. You provide us with all our needs. We are forever grateful. Lead us, Lord, to walk with integrity and with peace in our hearts. Let our light shine ever so brightly that others may see your good works in us. Shield and protect us from evil. Restore health to the sick. Share your heavenly blessings to all who love you wholeheartedly. We praise your holy name. We praise your sovereignty. Let the peace of Christ rule in our hearts in all that we do. Forgive us, Father of our sins. In Jesus's name, we pray. Amen.

Pray from the Heart

Your prayer to God does not have to follow a particular formula. Although, it must be in God's will, for the right reasons and with no doubts. I will discuss this in an upcoming section. Praying to our Heavenly Father is not some dreadful task you have to do; prayer is a privilege.

If your prayer truly comes from the heart, it will reach the ear of God. John Bunyan once said, "In prayer it is better to have a heart without words than words without a heart." Your prayer does not have to be long-and drawn-out; short prayers are just as effective. You can say, "God, I messed up. I do not know what I was thinking. Please forgive me." Just a few words, like, "Lord, forgive me," is prayer in itself.

I prayed the wrong way for years because I sought my own will instead of seeking His. Each time after my prayers went an unanswered, I would attempt to make it better than before. Not all my prayers were answered, of course, but most were. I wanted to pray to Him and seek His will.

Praying to our Heavenly Father is something we should want to do. The fact about anything we are uncomfortable with is the more you practice, the better you become at it. Praying to God is not limited to a specific time, though where we pray can matter. It is better to do it in a private place. God wants us to call upon Him. We have the freedom to choose to pray at any time, and we should take advantage of it. The more you pray, the closer you are to God.

When and Where to Pray

When should I pray? Anytime you want to because that is what God desires. God gives us permission to come to Him and pray at will. We can pray in the shower, in the car, in the gym, or in the grocery store. We can say this, "God, please bless me this day. Keep evil and wickedness from my family and me. Thank you for all that you have given to us. Forgive me of my sins, in Jesus's name. Amen". His ears are open to the righteous, born again Christians who have accepted Jesus Christ as their savior.

There is never a wrong time to go to God in prayer. Do it silently in your mind while on an elevator, "Lord, be with these parents whose child is in critical condition and is on a breathing machine. Give the medical staff strength and knowledge to heal that sweet little baby. You can do all things. In Jesus's name. Amen". I'll let you in on a little secret. There's a saying my father used to say, "It is best when you pray for and bless others."

There is never a time when we cannot pray to God. We cannot say that God is too busy; we will pray tomorrow. He always has time for us. The prayer line is never closed. It is open to communicating with Him anytime. There is no prayer too great for God, nor is there no prayer too small. You can say, "Thank you God. Amen." He desires for our hearts to be open to Him. God wants us to be near to Him in prayer, and by being close to Him, we create an intimate relationship.

Quiet Time

Becoming close to God in prayer means leaving behind all the excess noise and interference that life brings. Noisy rooms are not optimal places for a spiritual connection with God. Mothers with small children will have to be creative when spending quality time with our Heavenly Father. A precious little one clinging to your every move can interrupt even regular bathroom visits. Try practicing prayer before your child goes to sleep. Mommy or daddy can say bedtime prayers to their children and enjoy the sweetness of watching them fall asleep. It is a good practice to develop your children's spiritual maturity. It will keep you on your biblical toes when they ask you umpteen questions!

Jesus taught us to pray in secret or in a private place. God wants the conversation to be personal. Outside distractions can disrupt your thoughts and your prayer to Him. Jesus also taught us to pray often. He would go early in the morning to spend time with God by Himself. Anytime you pray to God is acceptable. Even so, morning prayers are your most effective time to talk to Him. That way, you'll start your day by asking for guidance and instruction. You ask Him to help you get through the most challenging times of the day too. Just pray to Him for strength and endurance.

Investing the Time to Pray

Your body requires energy to get you through the day. You eat breakfast to give you physical endurance. So, you should also feed your spiritual needs. Begin your day by praying to God and reading the Bible. Before you read the Bible, ask God to help you apply the scripture to your life. Ask him for help in understanding it.

Do not make excuses such as, *"I don't have that much time in the day."* If you are watching some T.V. program late at night, change your habits. Go to bed earlier and get up earlier so you will have time in the day to spend with God.

I used to say the same thing, *"I don't have that much time."* I did not realize what I was implying until I did. A. W. Tozer said, "The man who would truly know God must give time to Him."

I found the time to spend talking to God and reading His Word. I learned more about God's time clock by building my trust in Him and having patience. During the time I waited on God's answer to my prayer, I learned to be patient. And during my patience, my trust in God grew stronger and stronger. It stemmed from my belief that He will do as He has promised to do. I learned to be dependent upon God in all that I do.

We get some understanding of God's timing from The Holy Bible. 2 Peter 3:8 tells us that one day is as a thousand years to Him. The Psalmist says, "For a thousand years in Your sight are like yesterday when it is past" (Psalm 90:4). God is not limited to time. His idea of time is entirely different from our concept. God is at the beginning of time and at the ending of time at the same time. God is the Eternal God—He is forever.

The point to take from this is to make time to talk to God in prayer regardless of how tedious your personal or business life may be. Invest five minutes of your morning communicating what is on your mind. Let Him take over from there.

You will be surprised how uplifting just a few minutes spent with God will make your day. A day that would be so much better than one without Him. Seek Him diligently from your heart, Ask Him to help you, and wait for His answer.

Previously nailed shut, windows of opportunity will suddenly become wide open. Miraculous healing that once seemed impossible becomes reality. The alcoholic loses the desire to drink, and the hardened heart becomes soft. The lost become found. The poor become prosperous, and failures turn into successes.

Believe this, my friend, the power of prayer can change things. Nothing is impossible with God when we are centered and focused on Him—praising, serving, and doing His will.

When we seek God's glory and His will above all things, seek the kingdom of heaven and all His righteousness, and demonstrate a godly and faithful desire, the spirit of prayer becomes active. "The prayer of a righteous person is powerful and effective" (James 5:16). The power of prayer changes things—God changes things.

Prayer pulls the rope down below and the great bell rings above in the ears of God. He who communicates with heaven is the man who grasps the rope boldly and pulls continuously with all his might—Charles H. Spurgeon

CHAPTER 2
Answered Prayers

"Ask, and it will be given to You; seek and You will find, knock and it will be opened to You. For everyone who asks receives, and he who seeks finds, and to Him who knocks it will be opened"—Matthew 7:7–8.

Abide in God

What is the secret to having God answer my prayer? Prayer is not a magic trick, which we may make on command—and poof! God does not take orders, and prayers do not work that way. Besides, magic is not real—prayer is! There is no secret, or anything hidden from you for God to hear or to answer your prayer. God wants you to communicate with Him with no secrets, constraints, or time limits.

We have the honor of praying to the Him, and He wants to give us everything our hearts desire. Although, as you will soon learn, God does request that our prayers to Him abides by His Word. Read the verse recorded by John, "If you abide in Me, and My words abide in you, you will ask what you desire, and it shall be done for you." (John 15:7).

The late Adrian Rogers said, "Prayers that get to heaven start with heaven." They start with heaven when God's Word is in our hearts. Our prayers to our Heavenly Father should be seeking His will in our life. They should be grounded in faith, balanced by belief and trust along with being for the right reasons.

Years ago, I would pray to God to get Him to see my plan. I had my agenda in life and prayed to God to make it happen. When plan A did not work, I went to plan B. There are twenty-six letters in the Alphabet. I probably went through them a few times. I was persistent in convincing God to adjust His thoughts on my plan, although He used these times to teach me. Thereby, He was changing my thinking in lines with what He had planned for me.

YOU ANSWER MY PRAYER

Dear, gracious, Father, your kingdom is forever and ever. You are the Almighty God. There is none like you. I praise and worship your holy name and love you wholeheartedly. I come to you today with a humble heart seeking your heavenly counsel.

Father, you know my heart that is always seeking you passionately. I desire to know you more intimately and to understand your good ways. Without you, I can do nothing. I cast all my cares upon you and put all my trust in you; I am anxious for nothing. You have planted me in a broad place and look after me and provide me with peace. You are always with me; You protect me under the shadow of your wings. Thank you, Father, for your divine protection.

I diligently walk in your Word, daily. It is the lamp that guides my feet and the light for my path. In all my ways, I acknowledge you. Through you, I have escaped the prison of bondage. I am not captive to anything that is not according to your holy Word. I am free of guilt, deception, pride, anguish, and sorrow. God, you have dominion over all things, and these things have no place in my life. I praise your holy Word, the sword of the Spirit, which demolishes any stronghold against you.

Father, your kingdom is an everlasting, and your dominion will endure forever. You are faithful to all your promises and loving towards all your creation. I claim your promises you have given to me. I hold them as treasures in my heart. I am convinced that nothing shall come between the unwavering-love you have for me.

Help me, Father, to be mindful of others. Help me to bear another's burden as I extend my hand to them out of compassion as you have shown me. I want to share the love you have given to me. Let the words from my mouth be those of truthfulness and righteousness. Let them speak of your never-ending love, grace, and mercy. Let my good works shine unto to others that I may be a blessing to you.

You are the Father of mercies and the God of comfort. Repair the hearts of the broken-hearted. Restore and bond their hearts with your everlasting love, joy, and peace. Promote wellness in those who are sick. Heal their bodies with your almighty power.

I praise your name in the morning. I praise it all day long. The meditations of your Word are locked in the bank of my heart. I am forever grateful for the blessings you have shown to my family and me; continue to bless us, Lord. Bless all your children who love you with all their heart.

Father, I have made my requests known to you. I also know you hear and answer my prayer. Thank you, Father, for your unconditional love. Lead me through the Holy Spirit that I may walk in obedience to do your will in my life. Guard and protect me from evil and deliver me from temptation. Forgive me of my sins. In your Son's name, I pray. Amen.

Live by Faith

"The just shall live by faith" (Romans 1:17).

A Broad Place

"I called on the Lord in distress; The Lord answered me and set me in a broad place" (Psalm 118:5).

Demolishing Strongholds

"For though we walk in the flesh, we do not war according to the flesh. For the weapons of our warfare are not carnal but mighty in God pulling down strongholds, casting down arguments and every high thing exalts itself against the knowledge of God, bringing every thought into captivity to the obedience of Christ" (2 Corinthians 10:3–5).

His Dominion Endures

"Your kingdom is an everlasting kingdom, and Your dominion endures throughout all generations" (Psalm 145:13).

Lamp to my Feet

"Your word is a lamp to my feet, and a light to my path" (Psalm 119:105).

Bear Burdens

"Bear one another's burdens, and so fulfill the law of Christ. For if anyone thinks Himself to be something, when he is nothing, he deceives Himself" (Galatians 6:2–3).

Father of Mercies

"Blessed be the God and Father of our Lord Jesus Christ, the Father of mercies and the God of all comfort" (2 Corinthians 1:3).

Requests Made Known

"Be anxious for nothing, but in everything by prayer and supplication, with thanksgiving, let your requests be made known to God; And the peace of God, which surpasses all understanding, will guard your hearts and minds through Christ Jesus" (Philippians 4:6–7).

Answered Prayers

It can be difficult to accept when God doesn't answer our prayers. We pray as earnestly as we can and with all our heart, but God remains silent. For most people, this silence could be a "No," or it could be a "Yes," but most take it as "Not Now." God is working out things behind the scenes. So, we must be patient. Not receiving an answer to our prayers can turn out to be in our favor. That's a fact that we learn in hindsight.

The Reverend Billy Graham explains it like this: "Sometimes God answers our prayer with a definite "No," and when that's the case, we shouldn't keep begging Him or demanding He give us a "Yes."

Remember: God loves us and knows far better than we do what's best for us. I can recall times in my own life when God said "No" to something I prayed for, and to be honest, I sometimes found this hard to accept. Later, though, I realized God's way was far better than mine, and I was thankful He had said "No."

Strangely, we may thank God for unanswered prayers, but that is not exactly what we want. At least, not initially. We want our prayers answered. I have learned that it is best to ask for God's will. *Is it God's will to be a blessing to someone? Is it God's will to share the gospel of Jesus of Christ? Does God want to bless His children abundantly?* These are relatively easy questions. God wants all those things. If I pray for you and ask nothing for myself, in return, I receive so many blessings that I lose count. Sure, we ask God for things for our personal lives. First, though, seek God's will, then you will have to find help in keeping up with your answered prayers!

Blueprint for Answered Prayers

1. We pray, seeking *God's will.* John tells us, "Now this is in the confidence we have in Him, that if we ask anything according to His will, He hears us" (1 John 5:14).
2. We must *believe* that God will answer our prayers. "And whatever things you ask in prayer, believing, you will receive" (Matthew 21:22).
3. Our prayer must be for the *right reasons.* "You ask and do not receive because you ask amiss, that you may spend it on your pleasures" (James 4:3).
4. We should pray in *Jesus's name.* "Until now You have asked nothing in My name. Ask, and You will receive" (John 16:24).

Our prayers to our Heavenly Father should be for seeking His will in our life grounded in faith balanced by belief and trust along with the right reasons. Lastly, we end our prayers to God, asking in Jesus's name.

God's Will
What is my purpose in life? How do I know God's will? What is God's plan for me? Our sole purpose in this life is to love the Lord with all our hearts,

and serve Him in obedience in everything that we do. God does not withhold anything from those who love Him wholeheartedly. Jesus gave us the greatest commandment of all, "You shall love the Lord your God with all your heart and with your soul and with all your mind" (Matthew 22:37). Assuming you follow this commandment, seeking God's will should be easy.

How do I know if the voice is from God or, if it is from my own thoughts I'm hearing? This is called discernment. Itis a learned skill taught through prayer and reading the Bible. God wants us to know what His will is for our life. One place to start is by praying to Him. Ask God for insight concerning His will for your life. Remember, the more you pray, the closer you are to God. You will be able to distinguish God's voice from your own by using discernment. It comes from being near to God, talking to Him as you would your earthly father, and reading the Bible. If you are new to reading the Bible or find it difficult to understand, I suggest that you start with the book of John in the New Testament.

Once you develop a habit of consistent reading, the words from the pages, mysteriously, become alive. It is not easy to explain. The best I can say is that the verses become God's voice. I know it sounds strange, but the truth of the matter is God's Word is alive (Hebrews 4:12)—it's powerful. Consistently reading of His Word changes how you think, feel, and act. Your vision and hearing become clear, so you'd be able to see and hear things differently. God's voice comes alive through His holy Word, even when we hear His voice through others. You will soon hear God speaking; God's voice is everywhere.

A likely source of God's voice could be through a godly coworker or a stranger at the grocery store. Pay attention to the details, especially if a conversation rings a bell in your mind. It may remind you of things you have requested from God. You could be getting your answer. Here is what God Word says to us: "For I know the plans I have for you," declares the LORD, "plans to prosper you and not to harm you, plans to give you hope and a future" (Jeremiah 29:11 NIV).

The first thing that should stick out to you on reading this verse is that God has a plan for us. And in that plan, He desires for us to be prosperous. He wants us to succeed in His glory. God wants to shower us with so many blessings that we lose track of how much he has blessed us. God promises to watch over us with His divine protection as He sets us on a journey that is specifically designed for us. The psalmist wrote, "Yea, though I walk through the valley of the shadow of death, I fear no evil; for You are with me" (Psalm 23:4).

Between mountains are valleys, which are in the shadows. In our life's journey, we may go through dark and scary valleys, but God brings us through them. He brings us to the other side. If you look at the sun, you'll see your shadow forms behind you. If you look at the Son, Jesus Christ, the shadow of death is behind you. By His blood, Jesus has conquered death. He will be with us every step of the way of our journey. Jesus will protect us and keep us from harm like a Good Shepherd does for His sheep. I would much rather go through the valley of the shadow of death with Christ than to be on the mountain without Him.

God promises to protect us from harm and to give us hope with the anticipation of good things. He promises to lead us on a journey with a bright and prosperous future. That is God's plan for you and me.

The world tells us that we do not need God to be successful. It says we need to develop a positive attitude. That having a strong will to do anything we want to do without God's help. However, we cannot compromise with what the world tells us. We live our lives based on what the Word of God tells us. Do not be misled by this carnal thinking; it is straight from the devil's playbook. He wants you to think that so that he can take you away from God. Paul tells us, "Do not be conformed to this world, but be transformed by the renewing of your mind, that You may prove what is that good and acceptable and perfect will of God" (Romans 12:2).

My friends, make the decision right now—if you have not already done so. Follow God's plan for your life. J. Vernon McGee tells us, "You can believe a whole lot of foolish things, but God doesn't want you to do that. He wants your faith to rest upon the Word of God." We can only do this if we refuse to be conformed to the world. If we let ourselves be transformed by the renewing of our minds in Jesus Christ. When we seek His will above all things, we will be successful and live a life filled with many blessings. God wants us to stand on solid ground with the understanding of His will for our life.

Calm Sea

Balanced Faith

On the night when the disciples were meeting Jesus across the sea, there was a horrific storm. The winds were boisterous, and the waves were crashing from both sides of the boat. In the distance, the disciples saw what appeared to them to be a ghost. Jesus was walking on water. He told the disciples not to be afraid. Peter asked Jesus to command for Him to walk on water. Jesus said, *"Come"* (Matthew 14:29).

Peter stepped out of the boat with a leap of faith and began walking on water. However, once he began to look around at his surroundings, he fell. Maybe Peter felt the over-whelming power of the winds from both sides and became scared, or maybe Peter put more thought into his surroundings rather than on Jesus. Once he took his eyes off the Lord, Peter fell into the water. That is what can happen to you too. When you take your eyes away from the Lord, you may begin to have doubts about your own decisions.

At times, I have been guilty of taking my eyes off of Jesus. I took the blinders off and perceived that my success was accomplished through hard work and perseverance. "Not so fast," as the longtime sports commentator Coach Lee Corso puts it.

We tend to take our eyes off of Jesus when things are going well in our lives. Every day is a day on the beach when things are going to plan. It's when we lose our focus on Jesus that the storms of life surround us. When we lose our focus on Him, we see our surroundings and become scared. Maybe we panic. Jesus never told us that there weren't going to be stormy days, but He did say He will get us through them. Jesus says to us, "Come to Me, all you who labor and are heavy laden, and I will give you rest" (Matthew 11:28).

Peter was the only disciple who risked stepping out onto the water. The other disciples sat still in the boat. God is asking us to make a bold step of *faith*.

It is better to go through the storms of life with faith in Jesus knowing that He will save us rather than to live with anxiety and fear without Him—get your feet wet! Get to that point where you risk stepping out of your comfort zone, "Get out of the boat",—and follow Jesus.

Jesus told us to have faith as small as a mustard seed—a speck of faith followed by belief and trust. Jesus assures us, "And whatever things you ask in prayer, believing, you will receive" (Matthew 21:22). Our vision in our life is sharply focused when we view through the "lens of Christ". With our eyes faithfully on Him, if you honestly believe in whom Jesus says he is and trust Him with your heart, mind, and soul, you can do anything

The Right Reasons

Many people have said to me, *Why doesn't God answer my prayers—or—Why doesn't God listen to me?* Most often, I learn that it's because they are praying for the wrong reason just as I was when my prayers went unanswered. I will discuss more on why God does not answer our prayers in an upcoming section. For now, the focal point is asking God for things for the right reasons. People who ask why God does not answer their prayers may be praying to Him for material possessions. Worldly things may be off the mark from what God has planned.

You may want God to bless you with a lot of money, so you can buy extravagant things. However, that may not be His will. He wants to bless you more than you can imagine so you can bless others, which may be according to His will. James tells us, "You have not because you don't ask God. When you ask, you do not receive, because you ask with the wrong motives, that you may spend what you get on your own pleasures" (James 4:2-3 NIV). God does not mind you obtaining wealth. He encourages it. Besides, He is the one who gives it to us. "And you shall remember the Lord your God, for it is He who gives you power to get wealth" (Deuteronomy 8:18). It is His money. God will answer your prayers if it is according to His will and for the right reasons.

Ask in the Name of Jesus

Jesus tells us praying in the name of Jesus is God's will. When we pray in His name, we ask in His authority and glorify and honor it. By asking "In Jesus's name" and in His authority, we are approaching the throne of God. Through our belief and faith in Jesus, God may be glorified in His Son. John records Jesus's words, "If you ask anything in my name, I will do it" (John 14:14).

Our prayer to our Heavenly Father should always be according to His will. We should have confidence that anything we ask is going to be answered. Our Prayer to God must be well-grounded in faith and the belief that He will do as He has promised. And when we ask God for things in our prayer, we should do it in the name of Jesus.

Waiting on Answered Prayers

I have prayed to God to help me handle certain situations throughout the day. I get an immediate response back from Him. When I am working on a task, let us say, attempting to repair a leaking faucet at home. I ask in prayer when I mess it up worse than it already was. I get an immediate response back on how to fix the problem, i.e., call a plumber. There are certain things I do not have to pray to God about. For instance, if I have a headache, the logical thing to do is take some medicine. If it is persistent, I might want to see a medical doctor. However, there are many things, which I cannot do by myself. I depend on God to help me in those instances. I need God, so I go to Him in prayer and wait for His answer.

The answers will not come in an email or something that is entirely straight-forward, although they could. Usually, the responses you receive are not the ones you want but are the ones you'd expect. The late Norman Vincent Peale suggested, "Ask for what you want, but be willing to take what God gives you. It may be better than what you asked for". You may pray for a big, fluffy dog, and God gives you get a Sphynx, a hairless cat. That would sure seem odd. Who would expect that? However, you might learn later that the big, fluffy dog is not as attentive and loving as you would have liked. That the cat is always at your side, snuggled under your arm nightly—something you expected from your pet. Maybe God knew something before you asked. I bet that He does.

Moreover, sometimes, you pray for something for months, and God does not answer. Until that one day, He does. It is as though God is saying, "You prayed for this and I have allowed it, but it is not what is best for you." God may allow certain events to happen that are not necessarily His plan for you to teach you life's lessons. God's methods are not like our ways; He works in mysterious ways.

Father Knows Best

The Regional playoffs were just weeks away. The Trinity Crusaders were considered favorites to be back-to-back State Champions. Since childhood, Joey and Charlie have played baseball together. They were coached by their dad.

Joey has been an All-State pitcher for the Crusaders for the past three years. H has been scouted by several Major League and many collegiate teams. Joey did not want to be distracted during His senior year with all the hype. So, he decided to wait until the season was over before making up His mind about his baseball career.

Charlie is the younger brother. He has been Joey's personal catcher at home and for the last two years with the Crusaders. Charlie has been living under the shadow of His older brother. Even though he is an outstanding catcher, something was missing in his life. He wanted the recognition that his brother had received. He pulled his dad to the side after practice one day and asked:

"Dad, what do you think of me pitching in a game?"

"You're not a pitcher, Charlie," his dad blurted out. "You're a catcher, always have been."

"I know Dad. You've always wanted me to be a catcher, but what if I want to be a pitcher.?"

The dad replied, "Son, there's not a better catcher in the state who can call three perfect games in one year. That's unheard-of son. Nobody but you and your brother have done that. You should be proud of that achievement".

Frustrated now, Charlie shouted, "That's all I ever hear. Joey did this. Joey did that. I feel like I don't matter. It's all about Joey anyway. What's the use of talking to you if you won't understand?"

Charlie's dad took off his ball cap and placed his hand on his son's shoulder, "Your brother could not have pitched as well as he does without you calling a good game. You're the only catcher I have that can stop his curveball."

"I know all that Dad," Charlie said, holding his head down, "I just want to feel important too, you know."

"Son, you are important; you are special to my heart. I would do anything for you. I love you; you know that. Pitching is not your thing. God has given you and your brother special talents. Both of you have excelled in the game of baseball. And for that, you should be grateful."

Weeks went by, and the Regional playoff was underway. Joey had pitched a shutout game while giving up only three singles. It was the bottom of the ninth inning with two outs, with the Crusaders leading 1-0. Due up next was their number three-hitter, who has two of the three hits allowed. The Trinity coach called timeout and walked to the mound to speak to his pitcher.

"I'm pulling you, Joey. Your pitch count is high, and I need you rested for the remaining games," He said as He looked down to an empty bullpen.

"You're kidding right," Joey said with disgust. "I got this guy. And besides, there's no one warming up in the pen, Dad. Who's going to pitch"?

"Son, you have to trust me. Your father knows best."

Joey nodded and said, "Okay Dad, I trust you," as he ran to the dugout.

"Charlie, change you gear and come up to the mound," their dad shouted.

A man in the crowd shouted, "What's the matter with you, Coach? The catcher can't pitch!"

"Don't listen to him. Just throw the ball like you do with Joey in practice," his dad advised his younger son.

"Dad, I can't," Charlie whispered.

"Charlie, you can, and you will. It's your time to feel important. Now, throw him your good stuff."

Charlie pitched wildly and in the dirt on four straight pitches. "Ball four," yelled the umpire. There was one man on first base with two outs in the bottom of the ninth inning, and the school's home run hitter approached the plate. Charlie completed his wind up, reared back, and threw as fast as he could. "Hit the batter. Hit the batter," shouted the umpire. Now, with two men on base, Charlie's dad approached the mound.

"Charlie, they have used all their clutch hitters. The only guy left has a weakness for high fastballs. He can't hit them. Keep 'em high in his eyes. You've got this."

Charlie pitched his first pitch. "Strike one!" Both runners advanced, but Charlie didn't seem to mind. He reared back and threw another high fastball. "Strike two."

"Come on, Charlie, you got this," Joey shouted from the dugout. "You are the man!"

Charlie looked over to his brother and touched his hat while wiping the sweat from his forehead. He stepped up to the mound, digging the perfect pivot point, and released another high fastball. "Strike three!

You're out," shouted the umpire. Joey was the first to jump on his brother after he won the game for them. All his teammates rushed the mound and congratulated Charlie.

Charlie hugged his dad and said, "That was awesome! Man, I can't believe it. I won the game." Then, looking somewhat puzzled, he said, "But Dad, we were going to intentionally walk their number three and four hitters anyway. You knew the only guy left on the bench couldn't lay off the high heat, and Joey's pitch count was getting high."

"Yeah, I knew," dad said. "I had faith in you son. I wanted you to feel important, and I gave you a shot at it."

Charlie was brought to tears, "Thanks Dad. That meant the world to me. But you know, I've realized, I'm a catcher, always have been."

Patience is the Key

In the Bible, several characters prayed to God and waited for an answer to their prayers. Moses stayed at Mount Sinai for six days, while Jeremiah remained for God's instruction for ten days. Daniel waited for three weeks.

One thing to learn is that God's timing is always right. God is Omnipresent—He is everywhere at the same time. He is at the beginning of the world and the ending of the world simultaneously. That can be mind boggling. As I have noted earlier, we somewhat understand God's time clock by developing trust and patience in Him.

Do not Throw in the Towel

We live in a world where we expect everything we want to be immediately at our disposal. We want the fastest internet, and we want our takeout food as quickly as possible. So, naturally, we'd want our prayers answered right away. Most of the time, our prayers are not answered as soon as we would like.

The problem we face is we do not wait for enough time for God to respond to our prayers. We give up too quickly—we stop praying—and throw in the towel. As a result, our prayer to God seems to have gone unanswered. Do not give up too easily or get discouraged. God is working out the details to answer your prayer. It may take longer than you expect. Keep your eyes on the Lord and wait for His response. The late Reverend Charles Hadden Spurgeon was once asked how he kept from getting discouraged. He replied, "I think about God every fifteen minutes." Amen to that.

Daniel prayed for three weeks, but God answered His prayer that very day. It just took it three weeks to get to Daniel. We may think we want an answer to a particular prayer right away. God thinks differently. There are times when we think God does not answer our prayers, and we begin to lose heart. God does what is best for His children.

Behind the scenes, God is working out all the fine details to your prayer. You may need a car big enough for a growing family. A few weeks later, after you asked God for a new car, a friend has a sports utility vehicle with low miles in a garage for the last six months and will sell it for thousands less than at a car dealership. You may have complained weeks ago that God hasn't answered your prayer, but what you did not know was that friend was out of town on a training seminar for the last two weeks. It's worth the wait now. God saved you an additional eighty dollars a month. What about that new home you have prayed for that was just listed on the market? The homeowner has accepted a job out-of-state and wants to sell it quickly. You now have the opportunity to buy a house for fifty thousand dollars less than the other home. You know, the one where the deal fell through without a logical explanation.

So, when something you pray for doesn't work, God may other plans. Be willing to accept what God gives you. Paul tells us not to give up, "And let us not grow weary while doing good, for in due season we shall reap if we do not lose heart" (Galatians 6:9). We should be persistent and keep praying with hope and anticipation that our prayers will be answered on God's timetable. Or, as Paul says, in "due season."

Practice from the Heart

A young man and a priest are playing golf together. At a short par 3 the priest asks, 'What are you going to use on this hole, my son?' The young man says, 'An iron, father. How about you?' The priest says, 'I'm going to hit a soft seven and pray.' The young man hits his iron and puts the ball on the green. The priest tops his iron and dribbles the ball out a few yards. The young man says, 'I don't know about you, father, but in my church when we pray, we keep our heads down.'[1]

I like to play golf. On the one hand, golf is an enjoyable game, and on the other, it can be a frustrating game. That's mainly because I am not good at it. I do not play enough to be consistent. To be good at anything, you must practice. For anything to be worthwhile, it requires time, effort, and practice.

Prayer is like golf. To be good at it, you must invest the time, put forth the effort, and practice. However, unlike the game of golf, the position of our stance, the pressure of our hands, or the place of our head are not prerequisites for a meaningful and powerful prayer life. We can stand and pray. We can pray sitting or on our knees. We can pray with our eyes closed and heads bowed. We can pray with our arms reaching the heavens. If we want our prayers to connect with Him, praying from our heart is the best position to reach the ear of God.

Straight from the Heart

I had a conversation with a gentleman several years ago. He told me that the longest distance in the world was from the brain to the heart. There is much truth in that statement. Our natural self is always in a defensive mode to protect us from the harms of the world. We are afraid to reveal the things secured tightly in our hearts. God, though is all-knowing. He already knows what is in our hearts and wants us to open our hearts to Him. A genuine spiritual connection with Him comes straight from the heart. God wants us to pour out our hearts to Him in prayer.

Jesus tells us not to pray in a boastful way or out of pride. "And when you pray, you shall not be like the hypocrites. For they love to pray standing in the synagogues and on the corners of the streets, that they may be seen by men" (Matthew 6:5). Jesus tells us to pray in private with God and not showcase our request in front of people. "When you pray. Go into your room, and when you have shut the door, pray to your Father who is in the secret place" (v.6).

Jesus informed us not to use the same things in our prayer. "When you pray, do not use vain repetitions as the heathen do … They think

---

[1] https://www.funny-jokes.com/funnygolfcartoon-trivia.htm. Golfing Priest.

that they will be heard for their many words" (v.7). Jesus gave us a model for Prayer (Matthew 6:9-13). He said when you pray, pray in this manner:

Model for Prayer

1.) Praise God
2.) Ask for your needs
3.) Ask for forgiveness
4.) Ask for protection
5.) Praise God

The Lord's Prayer

"Our Father in heaven, hallowed be your name. Your kingdom come. Your will be done on earth as it is in heaven. Give us this day our daily bread. And forgive us our debts, as we forgive our debtors. And do not lead us into temptation, but deliver us from the evil one. For yours is the kingdom, and the power, and the glory, forever. Amen" (Matthew 6:9–13).

Praise God

You give all the honor, praise, and glory to God. Address your prayer to the Father. Jesus started His Prayer thus, "Our Father in heaven, hallowed be your name ... "Another example: "Heavenly Father, the earth and all its fullness are yours for you are the Creator of all things; You are an awesome God; you are good all the time. There is none greater than you Lord".

Ask for Your Needs

Ask for the things you need. Example: "Give us this day our daily bread ... "Another example: "Grant my family and me many blessings; secure us with the warmth of your comforting and unfailing love. Promote wellness to those who are sick, heal them with your mighty hands."

God knows we need things. He wants us to ask Him for them if it is according to His will. God already knows what you need; you must ask Him to bless you. God loves persistence. God is not a hard-nosed type of God; He's a loving God who wants to bless His children. Keep asking the Lord to bless you.

Ask for Forgiveness of Sins

"Forgive us our debts as we forgive our debtors …" "Forgive me of my sins in Jesus's name". God hears all prayers, but not all prayers are answered. If we do not ask for forgiveness of our sins, God does not respond to our prayer. Sin is like a contagious virus; it repulses Him. God hears the prayers of the righteous. We become righteous by accepting and believing in Jesus Christ. Through Him is the only way we are accepted by God.

Through our mediator, Jesus Christ, we are made righteous to God, and our sins are forgotten. They are lost in the sea of forgetfulness, never to return. What you did five minutes or five years ago is gone forever when you ask for forgiveness in Jesus's name. Do not keep bringing up some sin you committed in the past. God has forgotten them, and you should know that He has forgiven you.

We also must forgive others. Do not have hate in your heart or hold grudges. The Bible informs us, **"But if you do not forgive, neither will your Father in heaven forgive your trespasses"** (Mark 11:26). An example: "Teach me to love and pray for my enemies, and for those who persecute and hate me for Jesus's namesake. Teach me Lord to forgive others as you have done to me".

Peter asked Jesus how many times we should forgive our brothers. Jesus said we should forgive them seven times seventy. The point Jesus was making is that we should not keep count. Forgive others as the Lord has done onto you. Ask for the forgiveness of sins in Jesus's name.

Ask for Protection

"And do not lead us into temptation". The devil is the one who tempts; God tempts no one. God will allow temptation, but only however much we can handle. "But God is faithful, who will not allow you be tempted beyond what you are able, but with the temptation will also make the way of escape, that you may be able to bear it" (1 Corinthians

10:13). "Deliver us from the evil one". Satan will take advantage of any weakness to lure you into temptation. Quoting Scripture is the best way to get rid of the devil. "Away with you Satan! For it is written, 'You shall serve the Lord your God, and Him only you shall serve'" (Matthew 4:10).

Praise God

End your prayer by praising God. "For thine is kingdom and the power and the glory forever. Amen". We are to praise God when we begin to pray, ask God for the things we need, forgiveness, for protection, and end our prayer by praising Him for His power and glory. Your prayer does not have to be in this order, nor do you have to pray a certain way. You only have to pray except in God's will. Jesus gave us the model of prayer. Our prayers to God serve a purpose: Through prayer, we are spiritually connected to Him. God is in Spirit; we pray in Spirit. We praise and worship Him, seeking His divine will. We raise supplications and ask for intercession and protection.

It's going to Rain

A farmer and his six-year-old son were plowing the field, preparing for the year harvest. The little boy said to his father,

"Daddy, why can't we just buy our food from the store like other folks?"

"We grow food and raise animals so our family and other folks can have food," the father replied.

"But Daddy, we didn't have any crops last year cause it didn't rain, and we lost two of our fat pigs and a cow."

It had been a devastating year after a six-month drought during prime harvest season. There was not enough food to sustain the animals.

"Last year hurt us pretty bad," the boy's father said, looking up to the sky, "But the good Lord willing, we'll be alright this year."

The puzzled little boy said, "You mean God wasn't willing last year?"

"The Lord is always willing," the man said with a smile, "He has His reasons. I'll pray more this year."

"Daddy, you pray every night at supper time."

The Father picked up his little boy and sat him on his knee, saying, "Sometimes, the good Lord allows us to have bad times so we can appreciate the good times."

The little boy looked up into his father's eyes, "Daddy, if I pray with you, do you think God will give us a good crop this year?"

"Yeah, He loves to hear prayers from the little ones," as he turned his head, wiping off tears, "You do that."

"Dear God, my Daddy says you love us a lot and he knows everything. Let it rain so the man in the fancy suit won't upset my Mama. Let it rain so we will have food to feed my pet pig, and for other people. God, let it rain for my Daddy. Amen."

The next day after he had completed his chores, the little boy put on his raincoat and ran as fast as he could to the field. He ran up and down the rows in the field shouting while looking up at the sky, "It's going to rain! It's going to rain!"

His father came out to the field, saying, "Why in the world are you wearing a raincoat? It hasn't rained in months and there isn't a cloud in the sky."

"Daddy, I prayed for rain. It's going to rain," the excited little boy replied.

The boy's father walked back to the house and met his wife on the porch. "Look at him. He's determined it's going to rain—he actually believes it's going to rain today."

"Yep," replied the wife, "he reminds me of you. You used to believe like he does. Sometimes, God uses unusual circumstances to tell us something. God is telling you to have faith and believe like our son believes."

The next day after no rain from the previous day, the little boy completed all his chores. Again, he put on his raincoat, and ran to the field. For hours and hours, the little boy ran up and down the rows shouting, "It's going to rain, it's going to rain."

It was nearing dark and time for supper. The little boy headed back to the house and told his father, "It's God's will Daddy. He wants us to have food to eat. He is going to let it rain for sure. I know."

And before the little boy could get his raincoat off, the downpour began. He ran outside, jumping with joy—"it's raining Daddy, it's raining. See Daddy? God does listen."

Walk by Faith

We can learn a lot from children. God's word tells us, "But let Him ask in faith, with no doubting" (James 1:6). The example of that young boy shows us that his faith was strong. He had believed it would rain and so, it did. The Bible tells us that, "We walk by faith not by sight" (2 Corinthians 5:7). We must believe that God will deliver us His blessings. We serve a loving God who wants to bless all His children. He does not want to withhold any good things from us if we are walking in obedience to Him and according to His will. God hears the prayers of the righteous. The author of Hebrews writes, "Now faith is the substance of things hoped for, the evidence of things not seen" (Hebrews 11:1). Be strong in your faith.

If you want God to rain down His blessings on you, you need to be living in a godly manner. You need to be walking in faith, believing that God will answer your prayer and bless you, without a doubt. God wants your whole heart to be devoted to worshipping and praising Him.

If you do all the talking when you pray, how will you ever hear God's answers? — A. W. Tozer

CHAPTER 3
When God Speaks

"I called on the Lord in distress; The Lord answered me and set me in a broad place"—Psalm 118:5.

When God Speaks

It's difficult to hear God's answer to your prayers when you are not one hundred percent focused on Him. God does not want just a piece of you—He wants *all* of you. He wants you to be communicating with Him through daily prayer. Reading the Bible and having daily prayers strengthens our relationship with God. It opens our hearts and minds to understand what He is saying to us. You cannot get a response to your prayer and discern whether it is from God or not without being in a consistent relationship with Him.

Some people who are not in an intimate relationship with God cannot distinguish what He is saying from their inner voice. It is an example of how misguided one may be by not having a close fellowship with God. I know this from my past experiences. I am educating those who do not know and reminding those who do but have been distant from the Lord. It can happen to all of us.

Certain people's way of thinking can be significantly distorted due to their self-centeredness. They can become deaf and blind to godly things. They get wrapped up in the things of this world that they lose focus on or depend on God until they are in an unwanted situation and need something. These same people are focused on what the world says. The problem is the world blocks out what God is trying to tell them. The world declares to them that they don't need God to be successful. It teaches a "Do whatever it takes" attitude to gain prosperity and success. They watch inappropriate things on T.V. and the Internet that their minds are so clouded with junk that they cannot hear what God is saying. These people can be misguided without God's counsel to the point of hardship and unwanted circumstances.

When you ignore the warning signs in your life, you could get into trouble. When you forget God, life will be trouble. At times, God uses unusual circumstances to answer your prayers. If you ignore your problems, you may suffer the consequences. If you are not close to God through prayer and reading His Word, you will not know what He is saying.

God's Voice

God uses His godly people to answer our prayers, although He may also use non-Christians to be His voice. God speaks to us through His divine nature. His voice is everywhere. In the New Testament, fifteen times Jesus has said, "For those who have ears to hear, let him hear". Tuning in to God's voice may take a little practice. However, by beginning a daily devotional and habit of praying to God, you soon will start to hear and understand what He is instructing you to do. You should make it a daily and nightly practice of reading God's Word and praying to Him.

According to Phillippa Lally's research in the *European Journal of Social Psychology*, on average, habits are usually formed around sixty-six days[1]. We all have habits. Make your reading your Bible and praying to God. Choose to follow God's plan for your life and follow His will.

You may also have many questions about dilemmas in your life. And you have not received answers from God. Who do you ask?

First, find a church home, if you do not already have one. A church that preaches the Word of God and the gospel of Jesus Christ. The pastoral team at your church has personnel who will counsel you in a Christian and godly way and guide you in biblical principles.

Second, get involved in a small Bible study group. They are an excellent opportunity to share your situations with other Christians. The ones who have gone through similar situations that you may be going through. They may have open ears in which you can release any unwanted feelings or troublesome issues.

Tune in to God

People may be at the lowest moments in their lives when they seek God for blessings. They may have problems with financial security, health issues, or emotional insecurities.

They can be so eager to tell God to comply with their every want and need that they do not tune in—they do not listen to Him. They are more concerned about whether God hears their prayers when they should be listening to Him when He answers.

I am sure, at some point, everyone has been guilty of blocking out God's voice. We probably did not do this intentionally. Nonetheless, unblocking God's voice can be done relatively easily. You cannot live in this world without hearing God's voice.

We will be able to hear God's voice when we learn how He speaks to us. God speaks to us through His Word, through prayer and by our circumstances. Be observant when strange events take place. They could be warning signs. Develop a high level of awareness to your surroundings, and if you're missing the cues God may be sending you, be ready for some other strange situation. Or God could use His voice to get your attention. Listen with attentive ears. As I have mentioned previously, not only does God use Christians to be His voice but also from non-Christians. Pay attention to all things. God may be answering your prayer.

Be Specific

A man wants a hole dug in his yard. He has a shovel and places it into the ground where he wants the hole. The man prays, "God, I need for you to dig me a hole." Nothing happens. Days go by, and the man prays again, "God, I need for you to dig me a hole." Still, nothing happens. A week later, the man's neighbor walks over and asks, "What are you doing with the shovel in the ground?" The man replies, "I prayed to God to dig me a hole." The neighbor says, "How big do you want the hole?" The man tells his neighbor, "I don't know, I just want a hole." The neighbor shakes his head and says, "Why don't you dig the hole?"

The man in the story lacks a few things. First, He doesn't have a plan. He doesn't know what he wants. It's like asking for a job with no reference as to what kind of job. Secondly, he could have dug the hole himself.

Avoid vague prayers—be specific. You may want a higher-paying job in the computer industry that has an excellent insurance plan for your family and offers a paid vacation. You may want to work for a company or an organization that values its employees and gives back to the community. You may want to work with people who not only love their job but are fun to be around. The main point is to give God all the details of what you want in your prayer—then act on them.

It takes effort on our part to get something done. We must utilize the things we have in front of us to make things happen. God may give you the means, but you have to put it into action.

The Lord's Sheep

We recognize God's voice when we are close to Him. Jesus told us, "My sheep hear my voice, and I know them, and they know Me" (John 10:27). The only way we will distinguish the voice we hear is from God is to be filled with the Spirit.

The writer in Hebrews 5:13-14 wrote some powerful words about the "Righteousness of Christ." Some people may be on milk as an infant. They are unskilled and inexperienced and are in the spiritual infancy phase. However, as we age with spiritual maturity, we eat solid food; we digest the Word of God. And through practice and discipline, we learn those differences between morally right and wrong. We can discern God's Word. As spiritually mature Christians, we see through the "Lens of Christ"—we see His righteousness. Amen!

Keying in to the voice of God takes practice. If we are walking our life in Christ with obedience and trust in Him, we will be able recognize God's voice. His Word says He hears the prayers of the righteous, and He answers prayers according to His will.

Some people may ask, *Do I need to pray to God to be more righteous so He can hear my prayer?* No. We cannot make ourselves any more righteous. We became right with God when we accepted Jesus Christ and became born again. We were made righteous with Him through the blood of Jesus Christ. It is not based on what we have done, but what Jesus did on the cross. And because we believe in what took placed at Calvary, Jesus dying on the cross for everyone's sins, we became righteous with God.

Listen to God

I was at a store one day, waiting in line at the cash register. A person, also in line, started a conversation. It was a conversation that was a bit awkward but awe-inspiring at the same time. He said, "Sometimes, the best things in life are those we have to wait for." I looked at him, puzzled. Surely, he was not talking about the motor oil he was about to purchase for his car. I knew he was not talking about motor oil. I said to him, "Yeah, I think you're right". Oddly enough, God gave me my answer through a stranger. W. A. Criswell tells us that, "God sends people into our lives just when we need them, to say the right word, His word, just when we need it." God was telling me, *"Not now, wait."* I was eager for a reply from God, and my patience was thin. However, God's timing is always on time.

LET ME HEAR YOUR VOICE

Heavenly Father, you are the Most High who can do all things. Mighty are your works, God of heaven and earth. I worship and praise your holy name and love you wholeheartedly. I come into your spiritual presence with an open and humble heart seeking your divine wisdom and knowledge.

Please show me your good ways and lead me along the straight and narrow path. Be the light that directs my path to walk in obedience to do your will, which you have predestined for me. Your ways are not my ways; your thoughts are not my thoughts. Teach me, Lord, to understand and follow you in a holy manner. Let me hear your voice so that I can know you more intimately.

Your Word says that you hear the prayer of the righteous. Teach me to listen when you respond to my prayers. Open my ears to hear your voice. Open the eyes of my heart to see your holiness and righteousness. Father, your Holy Word teaches me that you speak through my circumstances. Help me see and understand what you are telling me to do. I can do all things through you, who gives me strength when I am weak. I am nothing without you.

Father, your grace and mercy that you have given to me are more than I could imagine. You send out your sweet mercy and it falls on me like summer rain. By your grace, I am covered and cleansed from my sins and by the blood of the lamb. Search my heart Lord for anything that is not acceptable to you. Purge my heart from any iniquity or any unrighteousness and saturate it with your truthfulness and kindness. Mold me to be more like your precious Son, who died on the cross to take my curse away, to give me blessings, and to give me life. I am forever grateful for the never-ending love you have for me.

Send financial blessings to my family and me. Shower us from your mighty and generous heart. Show abundant blessings to those who reverently fear and love you with their whole hearts. You do not withhold any good thing from those who diligently seek you.

Father, teach me to love and to forgive those who have wronged me. Your Word says that you will forgive me if I forgive others. Help me to not hold on to grudges or have bitterness in my heart. Free me from anything harmful, and let your loving-kindness generate a new steadfast spirit within me.

I know my prayer to you changes things. Heal the broken-hearted; restore love, joy, and peace to those who are not near to you in their hearts. Draw them near and change their ways to follow you. Promote wellness to the sick; heal them with your mighty hands. Lift the spirits of those who are lost and need your love and compassion. Father take my hand and extend it to those who need your touch. Let my light shine to all people to see your good works in me. And let my heart be filled with the peace of Christ in all that I do. Deliver me from temptation and shield me from evil and wickedness. Thank you, Father, for hearing and answering my prayer. Forgive me of my sins.

In Jesus's holy name.

Amen.

Let Your Light Shine

"Let your light so shine before men, that they may see your good works and glorify your Father in heaven" (Matthew 5:16).

With All Your Heart

"Then you will call upon Me and go and pray to Me, and I will listen to you. And you will seek Me and find Me, when you search for Me with all your heart. I will be found by you" (Jeremiah 29:12–14).

God Knows the Heart

"Every way of a man is right in His own eyes, but the Lord weighs the hearts" (Proverbs 21:2).

Live by Faith

"For I am not ashamed of the gospel of Christ, for it is the power of God to salvation for everyone who believes, for the Jew first and also for the Greek. For in it the righteousness of God is revealed from faith to faith; as it is written, "The just shall live by faith" (Romans 1:16–17).

His Divine Power

"Grace and peace be multiplied to you in the knowledge of God and of Jesus our Lord, as His divine power has given to us all things that pertain to life and godliness, through the knowledge of Him who called us by glory and virtue, by which have been given to us exceedingly great and precious promises, that through these you may be partakers of the divine nature, having escaped the corruption that is in the world through lust" (2 Peter 1:2–4).

His Dominion Endures

"Your kingdom is an everlasting kingdom, and Your dominion endures throughout all generations" (Psalm 145:13).

Lamp to my Feet

"Your word is a lamp to my feet and a light to my path" (Psalm 119:105).

Bear Burdens

"Bear one another's burdens, and so fulfill the law of Christ" (Galatians 6:2).

Father of Mercies

"Blessed be the God and Father of our Lord Jesus Christ, the Father of mercies and the God of all comfort" (2 Corinthians 1:3).

Requests Made Known

"Be anxious for nothing, but in everything by prayer and supplication, with thanksgiving, let your requests be made known to God; And the peace of God, which surpasses all understanding, will guard your hearts and minds through Christ Jesus" (Philippians 4:6–7).

YOUR EVERLASTING BRIGHTNESS

Heavenly Father, you are an awesome God who deserves all the glory, praise, and honor. Your kingdom is forever and ever. Open the eyes of my heart to see your goodness and righteousness. Lead my life with your everlasting brightness to shine ever so brightly that others may see your good works in me.

Grant me wisdom to understand your perfect ways and give me discernment to hear your voice. Lead and direct my steps through the Holy Spirit to do your will. Give me the insight to follow your plan you set for me, that I may be acceptable to you.

Father, forgive me for my transgressions. Deliver me from evil. Place a hedge of protection around my family and me and show us abundant blessings. Thank you, Father, for your grace, love, and mercy. All this I ask in Jesus's holy name. Amen.

It's God's Story

Think of it like this, it's God's story, and we are a part of it. Seek God as though He is your best friend, He is by the way, and serve Him according to His purpose. When you notice unusual things popping up out of nowhere, pay attention to them. Nothing happens by accident. With God, there is always a purpose—everything is significant to Him. You must listen and trust Him when He speaks to you. God has great plans for you and me. Listen to Him intently; God may be telling you something.

Do not get discouraged when you do not get an answer right away. It may be days, weeks, or months before you get an answer to your prayer. Stay focused with your eyes on God and have patience. If you are seeking God's will, have confidence that He will answer your prayer. God will speak to you on His timetable. The apostle Paul encourages us by saying, "Being confident of this very thing, that He who has begun a good work in you will complete it until the day of Jesus Christ" (Philippians 1:6).

LIFT MY SPIRITUAL LIFE

Dear Father, I come to you requesting your divine guidance in my life. You are my rock and shield. I need your strength. Your Word says that in my weakest moments, I am strong in you. You give me the endurance to handle all things. Lift my spirit, and calm my soul with the warmth of your love.

Help me stay focused on you and to have good habits like reading your holy Word. Direct my steps to walk in the Holy Spirit full of love, joy, and peace. Lift my spiritual life to think of holy things and not worldly things. Keep me from temptation. Keep me far from evil and wickedness but surround me with your goodness. Let the fire in my heart shine for all to see your good works in me. I love you wholeheartedly. Thank you, Father, for hearing my prayer. Forgive me of my sins. In Jesus's name, amen.

Let God Work

When you attempt to go with your plan in life on your own, you will inevitably mess it up every time. Keep doing what you have been doing without God's counsel and guidance, and you will keep getting what you have been getting—disappointments.

If you adjust your life according to your plan, it will not work. If your plan is not working, it is because it should not be about your plan. When you choose your plan, you say to God, "I got this. I don't need you." When you decide not to follow God, you are making unwise decisions. I can attest to many heartaches that stemmed from such decisions. Leading your own life without God's direction does not make you a terrible person. However, it does make you a person who does not obey God. You will be in a constant tug of war with yourself, dealing with heartaches and misery.

The battle between yourself and God is easy. Give up trying to work a plan that you attempt to create, and let God work out the plan He has designed for you. God has a plan for me, and He has a plan for you. Let God work the plan He has created for you, and by doing so, you will understand what your objective is. You will know what God has designed for you by having faith that He will do what He has promised—and by trusting and obeying Him.

In a previous chapter, we have reviewed when God answers our prayers:

1. We pray, seeking *God's will*. John tells us, "Now this is in the confidence we have in Him, that if we ask anything according to His will, He hears us" (1 John 5:14)
2. We must *believe* that God will answer our prayers. "And whatever things you ask in prayer, believing, you will receive" (Matthew 21:22).
3. Our prayer must be for the *right reasons*. "You ask and do not receive because you ask amiss, that you may spend it on your pleasures" (James 4:3).
4. We should pray in *Jesus's name*. John records Jesus saying, "Until now you have asked nothing in My name. Ask, and you will receive, that your joy may be full" (John 16:24).

Hinders of Prayer

When we do not receive an answer to our prayer as quickly as we would like or not at all, praying to God can be disappointing and sometimes frustrating. You ask yourselves, *What am I doing wrong? Why does not God answer me?* Think of it like this: If you are in a traffic jam on the highway, it is usually caused by a car accident further up the road. The car accident blocks traffic flow, resulting in delays and frustration. Your prayer may be blocked, causing a delay. Or there may be something completely blocking or hindering your prayer. See the 4-points below for what may hinder your prayer:

1. Not seeking God's will (1 John 5:14)
2. Unconfessed sins. (Isaiah 59:2)

3. Resentment and unforgiving behavior toward others
4. Doubts

Not Seeking God's Will

Silence from God may be a hard thing to accept, especially over long periods. Unanswered prayers will cause us to ask many questions. *Are my prayers to God according to His will?* If your prayers are according to God's will, He will answer on His timetable. If they are not, they may not be answered. I call myself an expert on unanswered prayers. I was good at not getting an answer from God. I was a failure at prayer until I learned what the key was to getting God to answer me. And my friends, that is to seek God's will in your life. I am not implying here that God answers all my prayers, although He may in due time. Read God's promise that He gave to us, "Now this is the confidence that we have in Him, that if we ask anything according to His will, He hears us" (1 John 5:14).

Unconfessed Sins

When the thunder rolled from the preachers' mouth, that made the pews of the church seem to vibrate. I remember from my youth it was as if the strike of lightning pounded down on the altar. "All have sinned and fall short of the glory of God!" That was a time when the hair of my skin rose to attention as God's Word was preached and resonated throughout His house. I developed a fear of the Lord. God spoke through the late pastor Louis Knight that day. The thought of having sinned against God made me feel horrible. I was not scared of God. I was disappointed in my obedience to Him. I wanted to be pleasing to Him.

Throughout all the years of being close to Him, I understood that God is not an angry or a hateful God when we are disobedient to Him. Although He may be disappointed in our actions, especially if we have sin in our life. God hates sin. It is a major roadblock to your prayer to God. It very well may be why your prayer has not been answered.

There is not a person on this planet free from sin. That is why God's greatest gift to us is Jesus Christ. He took on our sins and our punishment so that we would be made righteous with God. That deserves a *"hallelujah and amen!"*

God's word tells us, "If we confess our sins, He is faithful and just to forgive our sins and to cleanse us from all unrighteousness" (1 John 1:9). If we have unconfessed sins, they separate us from God. Our prayers, most likely, will not be answered (Isaiah 59:2). "He who covers His sins will not prosper, but whoever confesses and forsakes them will have mercy" (Proverbs 28:13).

The Bible tells us that our sins were paid for through the blood of Jesus Christ. "For He made Him who knew no sin to be sin for us, that we might become the righteousness of God in Him" (2 Corinthians 5:21). Even when our sins are forgiven through Jesus Christ, God still wants us to repent and confess our sins against Him. Unconfessed sin blocks your prayers to God. He does not want anything to do with sin. It is against His divine nature. Confess your sins in prayer and ask for forgiveness in Jesus's name.

Not Forgiving Others

Jesus Christ paid the price when He died on the cross for our sins, thereby giving us forgiveness. It is the greatest gift God gave to us— His grace. God's grace has rained down on us, washing us from all unrighteousness through the blood of Jesus Christ. He expects that we show the same grace unto others by forgiving those who have wronged us. Jesus said, "And whenever you stand praying, if you have anything against anyone, forgive Him, that your Father in heaven may also forgive you your trespasses" (Mark 11:25).

Forgiving those who have wronged you may not be an easy step. Even so, it is God's commandment, and you want to be pleasing to Him. Forgiving someone who did something wrong to you does not mean that you must also accept it to be right. You forgive because God wants you to. It's not saying, *"I'm okay with what you have done to me, let me be your door mat"*. Not at all.

When you truly forgive someone from the heart, it lets loose the toxic junk that has been weighing you down. Immediately, you begin to feel good about yourself. That' because you are not holding on to those things that harmed your physical health as well as with your relationship with God. God wants you to let go.

Holding on to resentments and bitterness for any length of time spreads throughout our body, causing all kinds of ailments. Sixty-one percent of cancer patients have issues with forgiving others, according to the research by Dr. Michael Barry, author of the book, *The Forgiveness Project*.[2]

Holding on to bitterness or having grudges against someone is not only poison to your body but also the death of your prayer. The gospel of Matthew records Jesus saying, "But if you do not forgive men their trespasses, neither will your Father forgive your trespasses" (Matthew 6:14–15). Remember, an unforgiving spirit blocks our prayers to God just as much as sin does.

When you have an unforgiving spirit, you will be trapped in cerebral imprisonment because of the guilt and anguish you have harvested. Forgiving others who have wronged you will release you from the emotional bondage. It will no longer keep your mind and body tied down. True forgiveness sets you free. You cannot say, *"I forgive you, but I'll never forget."* God wants you to love all people and be forgiving. God wants us to forgive others as He forgives.

Doubting

Our prayers will be hindered if we do not believe God will answer them. Jesus's half-brother, James, tells us, "But let him ask in faith, with no doubting" (James 1:6). Faith is believing in something when it is not physically in front of us—we cannot see it. "Now faith is the substance of things hoped for, the evidence of things not seen" (Hebrews 11:1). You must believe in your heart with no doubting. Have faith that God will provide and answer your prayer. Faith comes through hope with the anticipation and expectation of good things that sustain us. It is the belief that God will provide for us.

Let's wrap all this together. Remember sin blocks your prayer to God. It is a sure death to your prayer. Ask for the forgiveness of your sins in Jesus's name when praying to God. Forgive others who have wronged you. Do not hold grudges or resentments toward others; it will block your prayer to God—forgive others as God has forgiven you. When you pray, do not have doubt in your heart. Believe that God will answer your prayer. And most of all, when you pray, seek the will of God.

*Prayer is putting oneself in the hands
of God—Mother Teresa*

CHAPTER 4
He Never Let's Go

"Fear not, for I am with you; Be not dismayed, for I am your God. Yes, I will strengthen you and help you; I will uphold you with My righteous right hand"—Isaiah 41:10

When God seems Distant

There are a few times that I recall feeling the closeness of God. I remember it was right after my father died. I was in the back yard, silently praying while grieving—and it happened! It was as though the wind was in slow motion, and I could grasp it. It was at that moment I knew God was with me. I felt the presence of the Holy Spirit, the one that puts "goosebumps" on your arms. There have been other times when I have felt the Holy Spirit with me, but none like this one. The Holy Spirit walked by me. His presence answered my prayer and let me know He was with me. It gave me assurance that everything was going to be okay. I felt peace in my heart.

There are those times when we do not hear God's voice. During these silent times, God is teaching us something about ourselves. Think of a tree during periods with no rain. It's roots go deeper into the ground seeking water. By doing so, the roots make the tree stronger able to withstand other droughts and able to withstand any storms that come. When God seems distant, we dig deeper into His Word. We become strong and able to withstand any storm. Our Christian roots become stronger.

There are times of prolonged silence when we must have patience and wait for God to respond to us. Patience is a virtue we are not born with and must learn. We live in a McDonald's society and the age of technology; we have been trained to get what we ask for and get it right away. Fast-food restaurants are competitive, striving for customer service and increased sales. Quick, timely service gives restaurants a competitive edge. Computer industries are making computers and other devices so advanced that people can have immediate access to the Internet.

Our prayer to our Heavenly Father is immediate access; however, the answer back to us may not be. When God does not answer our prayers when we want Him to, we feel discouraged. We pray and pray with no answer; we begin to lose hope. Some people may ask themselves; *Does God even hear my prayers? Does He love me? Am I such a bad person? What am I doing wrong?*

God is Omniscient

We may feel that God has abandoned us during long periods of silence. We also may think that He does not hear anything we say. We get disgruntled and quit praying. First and foremost, God will never abandon us—Never. Secondly, God hears everything. God knows everything. The Bible says, "For the eyes of the Lord are on the righteous, and His ears are open to their prayers" (1 Peter 3:12).

Take this point to heart, lock it there, and throw away the key—sin separates us from God. It is our sin that alienates us from God, and causes Him to seem distant. Do you have unconfessed sins? If so, this is may be the reason God seems distant. The Bible tells us that once we were far from God, but through Jesus Christ, we are close to God (Ephesians 2:13). Jesus Christ is the only link between God and our sin. We must ask for forgiveness of our sins.

HUMBLY PROCLAIMING

Dear Heavenly Father, you are the Almighty God that is gracious and loving. I worship and praise your holy name and love you with my whole heart. I come to you humbly proclaiming your honor, glory, and majesty.

Purge my heart Father and take away any unrighteousness within me. Lock your Word in the bank of my heart. Mold me to be more like your precious Son. Saturate my mind and soul with holy things. Open my eyes to see your truthfulness and righteousness.

When I get angry, you say, be still and do not sin. When I am anxious, you tell me not to worry; when I feel afraid, you tell me you will never leave me nor forsake me; you are always by my side upholding me with your righteous right hand. You are always faithful to your Word. You lead me beside the still waters and restore my soul.

I am a sinner, and I am nothing without you in my life. You are the light that brightens my path. Nothing can take away the love you have for me. Your grace is sufficient as it pours down on me from the heavens. By the blood of the precious lamb and my savior, Jesus Christ, you cleanse me and wash me white as snow. Take my transgressions and throw them into the sea of forgetfulness.

Lite the lamp in my soul with a never-ending fire fervently spreading the good news to all people, that our Lord Jesus Christ is alive and is coming back soon, whoever believes and accepts Him will have everlasting life. Please create a new steadfast spirit within me to stand up against anyone or anything against you. Place a hedge of protection around me from evil and wickedness. Deliver me from the wiles of the evil one. Guide and direct my steps through the Holy Spirit that I may walk in obedience to do your will.

Grant my family and myself many blessings. Secure us with the warmth of your comforting and unfailing love. Promote wellness to those who are sick. Heal them with your mighty hands, and comfort the families of those who may be in your presence soon. Strengthen our hearts to withstand the storms of this world. Open the hearts of nonbelievers that you wish no one to perish but to have everlasting life. Thank you, Father, for your never-ending love, grace, and mercy and for hearing my prayer. Forgive me of my sins. I ask this in the name of Jesus. Amen.

Walk in the Light

"But if we walk in the light as He is in the light, we have fellowship with one another, and the blood of Jesus Christ His Son cleanses us from all sin" (1John 1:7).

Through His Blood

"In Him we have redemption through His blood, the forgiveness of sins, according to the riches of His grace, which He made to abound toward us in all wisdom and prudence" (Ephesians 1:7–8).

Let Your Light Shine

"For it is God who works in you both to will and to do for His good pleasure. Do all things without complaining and disputing, that you may become blameless and harmless, children of God without fault in the midst of a crooked and perverse generation, among whom you shine as lights in the world" (Philippians 2:13–15).

The Armor of God

"Put on the whole armor of God, that you may be able to stand against the wiles of the devil" (Ephesians 6:11).

Led by the Spirit

"For as many as are led by the Spirit of God, these are sons of God. For you did not receive the spirit of bondage again to fear, but you received the Spirit of adoption by whom we cry out, "Abba, Father." '(Romans 8:14–15).

God Hears the Righteous

"For the eyes of the Lord are on the righteous, and His ears are open to their prayers" (1 Peter 3:12).

AN AWESOME GOD

Heavenly Father, I come to you today, humbly proclaiming your majesty and holiness. You are an awesome God who is good all the time. I praise your holy name seeking your divine counsel.

Guide my steps through the Holy Spirit to be more acceptable to you and to do your will. Lead and direct my life to become more like Jesus. Open the eyes of my heart so that I can see your good ways. Saturate your holy Word into my heart that I may know you.

You knew me before I was born, watched me grow, and say I am wonderfully made. You are a loving God. Your love for me is more than I can imagine. I love you with my whole heart. You stretch out your mighty hands with an abundance of grace, love, and mercy. Father, your grace falls on me like precious rain cleansing me with the blood of the lamb from any unrighteousness. Thank you for being a merciful God.

I have called out to you daily, and you hear my cry and answer me. I need you, Lord. I am nothing without you. I may fall short, but you always hold me up. Your Word tells me that you will never leave me nor forsake me. You are faithful to your promises. I am convinced that no man can tell me otherwise that you are always beside me helping me with your righteous right hand. Let my walk in Christ, my countenance, shine ever so brightly that people see your light in me.

Father, you shield and protect me from harm. When the evil one knocks on the door of my heart, you tell Him you live here, and he goes away. No evil, no flesh, no principality can ever separate the love you have for me. Thank you for your divine protection.

Teach me to show kindness and lovingness to a world filled with hate. Teach me, Father, to extend a hand to those in need, as you have shown to me. Teach me to forgive others who have harmed me like you, also shown forgiveness to me. Lead your disciples with boldness and courage to spread the gospel of Jesus Christ that all who accept and believe in Him shall have everlasting life. Give faith to nonbelievers and open their hearts that you wish no one to perish but live eternally in your kingdom.

I pray that you will lift the broken-hearted. Comfort and bless them with your unfailing love. Promote wellness to those who are sick. Heal their bodies with your mighty hands. Give to those who fervently seek you. Show abundant blessings to all your children who reverently fear you.

Father, you are worthy of all praise and glory. You give me the strength to withstand any storm. I can do all things through you. I am forever grateful for the blessings you have given to my family and me. Continue to bless us, Lord. Let the peace of Christ rule in my heart in all that I do. Thank you, Father, for your love, grace, and mercy. Deliver me from temptation. Forgive me of my sins in Jesus's holy name. Amen.

God is Great
"Therefore You are great, O Lord God. For there is none like You, nor is there any God besides You" (2 Samuel 7:22).

Power, Glory, Victory, and Majesty
"Yours, O Lord, is the greatness, the power and the glory, the victory and the majesty; For all that is in heaven and in earth is Yours; Yours is the kingdom, O Lord, and You are exalted as head over all" (1 Chronicles 29:11).

Grace and Glory
"For the Lord God is a sun and shield; The Lord will give grace and glory; No good thing will He withhold from those who walk uprightly" (Psalm 84:11).

Love Your Enemies

"You have heard that it was said, 'You shall love your neighbor and hate your enemy.' But I say to you, love your enemies, bless those who curse you, do good to those who hate you, and pray for those who spitefully use you and persecute you, that you may be sons of your father in heaven; for He makes His sun rise on the evil and on the good, and sends rain on the just and on the unjust" (Matthew 5:43–45).

Flee from Temptation

"Blessed is the man who endures temptation; for when he has been approved, he will receive the crown of life which the Lord has promised to those who love Him" (James 1:12).

THE MOST HIGH

Heavenly Father, you are the Most High who deserves all glory and honor. You are worthy of being praised. You are the almighty God who can do all things. Nothing is impossible with you. I worship and praise your holy name and love you with my whole heart. I come to you with an open heart on bended knees with arms raised toward the heavens seeking your divine guidance.

You have put joy in my heart and bounce to my steps. Lead me, Father, in your righteousness, and make your way straight within me. Direct me through the Holy Spirit to walk in obedience to do your will.

Father, you are my rock and my shield. You are my fortress and my deliverer. Nothing shall come against me because you protect me with the shadow of your wings. I can do all things through you; I put all my trust in you. When I am weak, you give me strength. When I am afraid, you are always beside me; you never leave. When I call to you, you hear my voice and answer me.

I am a sinner. Forgive me, Lord. Wash away my iniquities and cleanse me from my transgressions in Jesus's name. Purge my heart from any unrighteousness and shape my life to be more like your precious Son. Fill my heart with your loving-kindness and your tender mercies. Teach me to love my enemies and those who persecute me for Jesus's namesake. Open the hearts to nonbelievers, because you wish no one to perish but to have everlasting life in your kingdom.

Lead me with boldness and courage to spread the gospel of Jesus Christ that all who believe and accept in Him will find salvation. Father show your abundant blessings to your children. Rain down your precious grace from heaven on us. Lift the ones with broken hearts.

Show the warmth of your love, grace, and mercy to all those who reverently fear you.

I am forever grateful for the blessings you have bestowed on my family and me. Nothing compares to the love you have for me. I give praise to your holy name. Deliver me from temptation and from evil and wickedness. Guard my heart with your never-failing love. Thank you, Father, for hearing my prayer. In the name of Jesus. Amen.

God is Patient

"The Lord is not slack concerning His promise, as some count slackness, but is longsuffering toward us, not willing that any should perish but that all should come to repentance" (2 Peter 3:9).

If you have not done so already, accept and believe in Jesus Christ as your Lord and savior. Repent from your sins, turn away from them, and accept Jesus into your life. Just say this prayer: "Dear Lord, I accept and believe that You are my Lord and savior. Come into my heart and cleanse me from any unrighteousness. Forgive me of all my sins. I ask in Jesus's name. Amen".

My friend, if this is the first time you prayed this prayer, the Bible tells us that you are royal family, saved through the precious blood. Hallelujah! There is a celebration in heaven going on right now.

Whoever Believes

"For God so loved the world, that He gave His only begotten Son, that whoever believes in Him should not perish but have everlasting life" (John 3:16).

A Prayer for Protection

"He who dwells in the secret place of the Most High shall abide under the shadow of the Almighty. I will say of the Lord, 'He is my refuge and my fortress; My God, in Him I will trust.' Surely, He shall deliver you from the snare of the fowler and from the perilous pestilence. He shall cover you with His feathers, and under His wings you shall take refuge; His truth shall be your shield and buckler" (Psalm 91:1–4).

Majestic Wave

He Never Let's Go

A little girl and her father were crossing a bridge. The father was kind of scared, so he asked His little daughter,

"Sweetheart, please hold my hand so that you don't fall into the river."

The little girl said: "No, Dad. You hold my hand."

"What's the difference"? asked the puzzled father.

"There's a big difference," replied the little girl.

"If I hold your hand and something happens to me, chances are that I may let your hand go. But if you hold my hand, I know for sure that no matter what happens, you will never let my hand go"[1] (Story by YJ Draiman).

God holding on to our hand always with love that our Heavenly Father has for us. No matter our circumstances, when we are not as close to God as we should be, He is always there with us. He'll never let go. Put all your trust in Him, and love the Lord with all your heart, mind, and soul.

Seek into your mind for approval that which is consistent with the Word of God. If by hearing you are convinced, you are a believer—Charles H. Spurgeon

CHAPTER 5
Saved through Faith

"So then faith comes by hearing, and hearing by the word of God"—Romans 10:1

Faith Comes by Hearing

There was a time when I placed more emphasis in my own faith in achieving my goals rather than what God had accomplished for me. Faith in myself led me on an emotional roller coaster with ups and downs, twists and turns that led to failures and disappointments. Something had to change—and it started with me. I surrendered my life to Jesus. I prayed for guidance and for God to increase my faith.

The faith to believe is given to us by God. Jesus mentioned it to us several times in the New Testament, "Those who have ears to hear let them hear" You must come to Christ with the intent to hear God's Word. You must have faith, belief, and repent of your sins. You must confess with your mouth that Jesus Christ was sent for your sins, died on the cross, rose on the third day, and sits at the right-hand side of the throne of God Almighty in the kingdom of heaven. The apostle Paul tells us, "So then faith comes by hearing, and hearing by the word of God" (Romans 10:17).

You cannot force yourself into belief—it only comes by hearing. Paul says, "How shall they believe in Him of whom they have not heard" (Romans 10:14)? Let no man tell you or convince any differently from that which God's Word says to you. "We trust in the living God, who is the savior of all men, especially those who believe" (1 Timothy 4:10).

PRAYER OF REPENTANCE

Heavenly Father, I have searched the high and low depths of my soul and find it unworthy of your unfailing love. I have cross-examined my heart, and it stands guilty in your eyes. Satan has poured vials of sin into my heart, filled with agonies and pangs. If I think for a moment, my deepest fear is sinking into the pit above my head, while the peaks and troughs drown me with shame. Like a sheep going astray, I transgressed to green pastures. Only to find nothing that could console the aches of my dry bones and the wet of my eyes.

Lord, your Word says that you are gracious and full of compassion. It tells us you are slow to anger but quick to mercy. Be merciful to me. You have given your only begotten Son to suffer and die on the cross. He rose on the third day, ascended to your kingdom, and sits at the right-hand side of your throne.

Jesus said He did not call on the righteous, but sinners to repentance. He said whoever finds Himself will lose it, but whoever loses His life for His sake finds it. Lord, I want to lose the person I never really liked, but to become the person I always wanted to be—and that is to be more like you. I need you, Lord. I am a sinner; I pick up my cross and follow you. You lift my burden and give me rest. You lead me beside still waters and restore my soul.

God, your Word tells me that I would live longer with the fear of you embedded within my heart. And my fear of you gives me an understanding for when I am weak; I become strong. My fear God does not hold back the flames of my rekindled heart, but through Christ, it strengthens me. Your grace falls on me like precious rain. My sins are washed away through Jesus Christ.

Father, your Word says your grace is sufficient for me. Through your sweet grace bestowed to me, I fall to my extremities with praise and thankfulness. Your greatest consolation you sent me, my Lord Jesus Christ. Because of my sins and my redeeming savior, I live and die in Christ. In Jesus's name, I pray, amen.

He hears Me
"The righteous cry out, and the Lord hears, and delivers them out of all their troubles" (Psalm 34:17).

Come to the Lord
"The Lord is merciful and gracious, slow to anger, and abounding in mercy" (Psalm 103:8).

Your Tender Mercies
"Have mercy upon me, O God, according to Your loving kindness; According to the multitude of Your tender mercies, blot out my transgressions" (Psalm 51:1).

Eyes on Jesus
"Fixing our eyes on Jesus, the pioneer and perfector of faith. For the joy set before Him He endured the cross, scorning its shame, and sat down at the right hand of the throne of God" (Hebrews 12:2 NIV).

Confess your Sins
"That if you confess with your mouth the Lord Jesus and believe in your heart that God has raised Him from the dead, you will be saved" (Romans 10:9).

"He who covers His sins will not prosper, but whoever confesses and forsakes them will have mercy" (Proverbs 28:13).

Pick Up the Cross

"Then Jesus said to His disciples, "If anyone desires to come after Me, let Him deny Himself, and take up His cross, and follow Me'" (Matthew 16:24).

He gives me Strength

"He gives power to the weak, and to those who have no might He increases strength" (Isaiah 40:29).

Wash Away my Sins

"I, even I, am He who blots out your transgressions for My own sake; And I will not remember your sins" (Isaiah 43:25).

God's Grace is Sufficient

"My grace is sufficient for you, for My strength is made perfect in weakness" (2 Corinthians 12:9).

Christ Who Lives in Me

"I have been crucified with Christ. It is no longer I who live, but Christ who lives in me. And the life I now live in the flesh I live by faith in the Son of God, who loved me and gave Himself for me" (Galatians 2:20).

Die Daily in Christ

"I affirm, by the boasting in you which I have in Christ Jesus our Lord, I die daily" (1 Corinthians 15:31).

What is Faith?

Faith is believing in something when it is not physically in front of us—we cannot see it. "Now faith is the substance of things hoped for, the evidence of things not seen" (Hebrews 11:1). Faith is what get us through the dark valleys of life, knowing God will get us through any situation. Faith is the covalent bond that strengthens marriages. Faith is knowing when we are without a job and the bills are piling up that God will provide provisions for us. It is the miraculous healing when doctors do not give us much hope; faith conquers the sting of death. Faith is through hope with the anticipation and expectation of good things that sustain us—it is the belief through faith that God will provide for us.

Moonlit Sea

WITH LOVING ARMS

Dear Heavenly Father, I love and adore You. I serve you with all my heart and worship your holy name. I humbly seek your good ways and divine wisdom.

You knew me before I was born, watched over me daily, and say I am wonderfully made. You know my heart. You know my past when I turned to my ways and was distant from you. Forgive me, Father. You accepted me back with loving arms and celebrated. Thank you for your unconditional love.

Through my adversity, you show me the right way to go. You teach me what is best for me. You do what a good Father does for His children. Forgive me for not putting all my faith and trust in you.

Father, when I pray to you and do not get a response, your distance seems like an eternity. I cannot even imagine what that would be like in your holy presence. You teach me things when I think you are not listening to me, but it is me who is not listening to you.

When I fail you, you do not give me what I deserve. You squeeze my heart until all the pride comes out and fill it with love, joy, and peace. You take away any selfishness within me and fill it with an overwhelming love for all people. You take away my frustrations and worry and soothe my soul with the warmness of your tender mercies and loving-kindness.

I am confident that no man or any presence will ever take away the love you have for me or the love I have for you. I am forever grateful for the grace that you have given to me as it flows down on me from heaven, washing my sins away.

Guide my hand to extend it to others in need. Open my mouth

to speak of things that are pure, honest, and of good report. Direct my steps to walk through the Holy Spirit to walk with integrity and obedience to do your will you created for me. Open my ears to hear your voice instructing me to make the right decisions. Open the eyes of my heart to see your good works and perfect ways.

I pray for those who do not have you in their heart. I ask that you draw nonbelievers near to you and comfort them with your gentleness. Help the ones who are lost in the sea of sorrow. Bring them out of the imprisonment of bondage that has held them captive through deception and lies of the evil one. Free them through the blood of the lamb, our redeemer, and our Lord and savior Jesus Christ. Open their hearts to find the way, the truth, and life in Christ Jesus. Take up their heartache and burden and give them rest. Give them peace.

Show abundant blessings to my family and me. Show your miraculous healing power by healing those who are sick, lead them to good health. Give jobs to those who are seeking employment. Guide those who are venturing into higher education endeavors. Demonstrate your compassionate, loving nature by blessing all those who seek you and love you wholeheartedly.

Father, you are the fire in my heart that drives my passion for living in righteousness and truthfulness. You are worthy of being praised, honored, and magnified forever and ever. Through you, I can do all things. Thank you for all the blessings that you have given to me. Guard and comfort my heart with the peace of Christ. Deliver me from temptation and from evil. Forgive me of my sins. Thank you for hearing my prayer. In the mighty name of Jesus, I pray. Amen.

The Lord is My Shepherd

Jesus told us that His sheep hear His voice and follow Him (John 10:27). Sheep feel safe when gathered in groups. They have a natural-born flocking instinct, although they need direction and guidance; sheep feel comfortable following a leader that they know and trust. Jesus is our Good Shepherd, our leader, whom we follow. Jesus told us the story of a hundred sheep where one sheep was lost. Jesus was not concerned with the ninety-nine (Luke 15:4–7). He is concerned with the one who was lost. Jesus said He did not come for those who were not sick but for those who are. He did not come for those having a savior; He came for those in need of one. Jesus said there would be a celebration in heaven over one sinner who repents than the ninety-nine who do not need to repent. If you have one leg on one side of the fence—Jesus is looking for you.

STRADDLING THE FENCE

Dear God, I have not prayed to you in a long time; I am sorry. I have lived the way I wanted to, and my life is terrible. I have ignored my family and friends, the ones who loved me. I turned my back on them, but they have not given up on me. They always tell me that they pray for me, that you, God, would change my heart and draw me near you.

I am at the weakest point in my life with nowhere to turn but to you. If you find in your heart God to forgive me for ignoring you for most of my life, I am willing to change. I believed in you all my life, but I was not religious. My family and friends tell me that you are always with me that you will never leave me. I regret that I did not put you first in my life. And for that, I ask for your forgiveness.

I have mountains of sins as they weigh me down daily. Take away my doubt, God. Will you forgive all my sins and make me a new person? I want to live the right way. Show me the way to live that is acceptable to you. I accept and believe that Jesus Christ is my Lord and savior. I want to follow Him. Forgive me of my sins. In Jesus's name, amen.

Growth in Faith

"Giving all diligence, add to your faith virtue, to virtue knowledge, to knowledge self-control, to self-control perseverance, to perseverance godliness, to godliness brotherly kindness, and to brotherly kindness love" (2 Peter 1:5–7).

Saved through Grace

"For by grace you have been saved through faith, and not of yourselves; it is a gift from God, not of works, lest anyone should boast" (Ephesians 2:8–9).

Faith in Christ

"That we might be justified by faith in Christ and not by the works of the law; for by the works of the law no flesh shall be justified" (Galatians 2:16).

We Understand through Faith

"But without faith it is impossible to please Him, for he who comes to God must believe that He is, and that He is a rewarder of those who diligently seek Him" (Hebrews 11:6).

Trust in the Lord

"Trust in the Lord with all your heart, and lean not on your own understanding; In all your ways acknowledge Him, and He shall direct your paths" (Proverbs 3:5-6).

THE DEPTHS OF MY HEART

Dear gracious, Heavenly Father, I give you all the praise, glory, and honor. Your throne endures forever and ever. I come to you on bended knee, proclaiming your name, seeking your divine counsel and wisdom.

You have searched the depths of my heart and have taken my sorrow and pain away and filled it with your joy and gladness. You have considered the requests of my supplications, and your ear is open to my voice. You enlighten my eyes to see your truthfulness and righteousness. You are my refuge in times of trouble. Without you, I am nothing.

Father, I ask for your forgiveness. I am a sinner. My sin is against you and only you. Through the blood of the lamb wash my sins white as snow. Purge my heart from anything that is not acceptable to you and fill it with your good ways.

Direct my steps through the Holy Spirit to walk in obedience to your will in my life. Give me discernment to hear your voice and give me wisdom and knowledge. Show your loving kindness with your righteous right hand. Guard and protect me under the shadow of your wings; Keep me in your secret place. Thank you, Father, for your divine protection.

I may fail you Father, but you never fail me. When I fall, you are always there to pick me up. You are always with me and will never forsake me. You hold to all your promises. Your Word is everlasting and proven. I am convinced that no one can take away the love you have for me. Thank you, Father, for your unconditional love.

Heal the ones who are sick. Demonstrate your miraculous healing wonders. Regenerate the warmth of your salvation to those who may have lost their way. Guide and direct their heart to hear your voice and draw near to them. Share your abundant blessings to all of those who love you wholeheartedly. Show blessings to all your children who reverently fear you.

I seek you all day long, Father, and praise your holy name to all to hear. You have put joy in my steps and poured love into my heart. I pray that unbelievers hear the good news that Jesus Christ is the only way to the kingdom of heaven. And that you wish no one to perish but have everlasting life. Father, I forgive those who have done wrong to me. Teach me to love my enemies and those who have hate in their hearts. Mold me to be more like your precious Son, Jesus Christ. Let my countenance shine upon all people, showing your good ways.

Thank you for the blessings you have given to my family and me. Keep me from temptation and deliver me from the evil one. Thank you for your never-ending love, grace, and mercy. Let the peace of Christ always remain in my heart in all that I do. In Jesus's name. Amen.

Tightrope of Faith

Believing and trusting in God balances the tightrope of faith. Jesus told us to have "Faith as a mustard seed … nothing will be impossible for you" (Matthew 17:20). Faith is having the confidence in God that He will do as He promised. Faith is praising God when things are going well and praising Him when things are not going well. When we believe in His Word and trust Him with all our hearts, we are faithful to God. We trust in Him by faith. We are saved by grace through our faith in our Lord Jesus Christ—we are given a gift from God.

Our purpose in this life is simple. We are to serve God and Him only. We are to be a good servant of the Lord. Listen to His instructions and be obedient to His commands without complaining. Put God first in your life and seek His will. Everything else will fall in place, the way God intended. Step out with a leap of faith, and let God control your life.

God is all-knowing. He knows your needs before you ask of Him. You may request a specific thing right away, but God may choose to wait. A good Father does what is best for His children. Be patient with God's timing, and always trust in Him. Be patient and keep the faith that God will do what he promised. Wait and listen for His voice. Never give up. Keep praying. Perseverance strengthens your Christian roots. Stand firm in Christ and be ready when God opens a door—He has big plans for you.

FORGIVE ME, FATHER

Heavenly Father, God of all creation, the only true living God, I come to you today seeking your forgiveness. On bended knees, I cry out to you, seeking your love and spiritual presence.

My heart aches from misery and sorrow. I find it hard to reach out to you because of the many sins I have committed. Please find in your heart to forgive me. I have done so many bad things that weigh down my heart. I need you, Lord. Change my ways to be the way you want me to be. Show me how I can be more acceptable to you.

Take my heart and squeeze out my sins that I have committed against you. Dry my eyes from my sorrow and disappointments. I try to increase my faith in you Lord, but it seems as though you are far away from me. Let me know that you are here with me. Let me feel the warmth of your love.

I do not know where else to go, but here on the ground, I kneel. Asking you to come to me and change my ways. Father, talk to me and let me know that you are always with me and never forsake me. Guard and comfort my heart under the shadow of your wings. Reach out your loving arms and embrace me with your unconditional love.

I confess that I am a sinner. I ask that you forgive me through my Lord and savior, Jesus Christ. Take my life and do as you will for your good pleasure. I am nothing without you. Lift my broken spirit Lord. In Jesus name, I pray. Amen.

The will of God will not take us where the grace of God cannot sustain us—Billy Graham

CHAPTER 6
Wherever God Leads

"May the God of all grace, who called us to His eternal glory by Christ Jesus, after you suffered a while, perfect, establish, strengthen, and settle you. To Him be the glory and the dominion forever and ever. Amen"—1 Peter 5:10–11

A Journey with God

Moses led God's people on a journey from the land of Egypt to the Promised Land. They resisted because they did not put their trust in God. Their lack of obedience and their lack of faith caused them turmoil and despair in the wilderness for forty years.

God may put you on a journey that may be uncomfortable. However, He did that with Abraham when God told him to leave his country and go wherever God sent him. God's words tell us that we walk by faith, not sight. Faith is seeing the "invisible". A.W. Tozer said, "You can see God from anywhere if your mind is set to love and obey Him." It is believing in something and trusting with all your heart. Abraham had God leading him. And God will do the same for you. You must have faith in God that He will guide and direct you on the path that He has designed for you.

How do you know if you're on the right path? We've learned from previous chapters is that you ask God in prayer. You simply say, "What is my plan, God?" or "What do you want me to do." You get direction from God through prayer and by being in an intimate relationship with Him. To have the relationship Abraham had with God, you must talk with Him daily. Even during the silent times, be persistent and keep praying daily. You can't be on and off with God—be patient.

God wants a personal relationship with you. Form one by staying close to God by prayer and reading His holy Word. As you begin to build a relationship with Him, God gives bits and pieces of His plan for your life. God gives you what you need to know. He does not reveal your entire life all at once. God gives you the perfect amount of information to get you started on your journey that He has designed especially for you.

When God leads you in a particular direction, you must follow it. He will not steer you down the wrong path or lead you into a problematic situation that you cannot handle. God wants you to follow His plan He has designed for you. The only way you can know what He has planned is by staying close to Him.

The million-dollar question that is often asked is, *How do I know if it is from God, or how do I know if it is from my own thoughts?* That is a valid question. One I have asked myself several times. Discernment is a learned skill taught by prayer and by reading the Bible. The first thing you must do is to ask God what His will is in your life be. After you have asked in prayer, wait on His answer. Be observant to your surroundings and listen intently. As you mature as a Christ-follower, with experience and practice, you will be able to distinguish God's voice as compared to your own by using discernment.

A Test of Faith

Sometimes, we go through stages in our life when we feel God is so far away us. His Word tells us that He is always with us, though. It is normal to feel this way during periods of silence. God has His reasons, even though our prayers are according to His will. He may be saying, *"Wait, not now."*

Another reason God may be silent is that He may be testing our faith. And do not think you are the only person who feels God is millions of miles away from you. Everyone has felt this way at some time in their life. It is a test in which we must remain firm in our faith. And through these trials and testing we gradually begin to change.

Life changes right before our eyes. At a moment's glance, the sky is smiling; at another, it is crying. Your life will not change overnight, your Christian roots will grow with each stormy trial making you stronger. Your journey might hurt at times. Once you have conquered any storm that life throws at you, you'll become like a tree with deep roots that can never be uprooted. Charles Spurgeon tells it like this, "Trials teach us what we are; they dig up the soil and let us see what we are made of."

Not all our days will be a beautiful, well-manicured rose garden. There will be thorns and weeds in our way. God never promised that our journey will be free from obstacles or trials nor has He promised that our life would be picture perfect, but God does want us to trust Him. At times, God allows us to experience periods of difficulty and sacrifice. We will face difficult challenges. What you do with is up to you.

The Bible calls this a time of testing, and it may include times of afflictions, suffering, and sacrifice. Billy Graham teaches us that "Suffering is a part of the human condition, and it comes to us all. The key is how we react to it, either turning away from God in anger and bitterness or growing closer to Him in trust and confidence". Here is God's promise to us when faced with difficult times, "May the God of all grace, who called us to His eternal glory by Christ Jesus, after you suffered a while, perfect, establish, strengthen, and settle you. To Him be the glory and the dominion forever and ever. Amen" (1 Peter 5:10–11).

God Knows Best

It is impossible to know the mind of God. The Bible tells us that His thoughts are not our thoughts, and His ways are not our ways. It also says His ways are unsearchable. God is Omniscient and all-knowing. He is Omnipotent and all-powerful, and He is Omnipresent, and everywhere. He is a Sovereign God. He controls everything. Nothing is impossible to Him, the Creator of the heavens, and the Universe.

There may be times in your life when everything you do seems to put you on the road to failure with hardships at every turn. When things in your life do not make sense, you ask, *Why is this happening to me?*

There have been times, many years ago, out of pure ignorance when I questioned God. I got the same response as when Job asked God why He let things happen to Him—nothing. In my experience, God doesn't respond to "why" questions. Think about it, He is the Sovereign God of the heavens and Universe. He is the Almighty God. The "why" questions should be directed toward us. Why should we question Him for what He does or does not do? It is better to ask, *What do you want me to do God? Where do you want me to go? Who do you want me to help?*

A Cross on the Ground

The late Reverend Adrian Rogers tells a touching story of a man who was at the lowest point in his life. "Aleksandr Solzhenitsyn was that brilliant Russian literary genius and dissident. Many of you have read [sic] after Aleksandr Solzhenitsyn, a brilliant and a godly man. But because he was a dissident, when Communism was so powerful, he was put into a prison camp.

Later he was released, and he told Senator Helms this story, and

Senator Helms told it to me. Solzhenitsyn said to Helms, "I hope you never know what real repression is." He told about how he was put into this labor camp, and they took from Him all books, all writing material. There was no radio. There was no television. There was no input from the outside world, and the prisoners themselves were not allowed to communicate one with another. All day long, laborious, backbreaking labor with Russian guards standing there, armed and ready to shoot anyone who tried to escape. Solzhenitsyn said this went on day after day after day. "I wondered if anybody even knew that I was here, much less did they care."

He said, "Finally, I decided that I would end my life. But," he said, "my faith would not allow me to do that. I knew it would be wrong for me to take my own life. But," he said, "my mind then became twisted and perverted." He said, "I had the idea that perhaps if I would try to escape, then they would shoot me, and I would not have taken my own life. They would have killed me." He said, "I know that was wrong, but my mind was twisted."

He said, "I found the day that I was going to do it. I was sitting under a tree. They'd given us a few moments from the work. I was sitting in the shade of a tree. I saw the Russian guard with His gun." He said, "I was ready to spring up. I'd almost put my hands on the ground, ready to spring up and run, to be shot in the back when," he said, "another man, a man that I'd never seen before, and perhaps I will never see again, perhaps was an angel, I don't know, but he came and stood in front of me. Remember, we were not allowed to communicate, not even to talk. But he looked into my eyes with a look of compassion and understanding, though not able to say a word." And he said, "He had a stick in His hand, a twig, and front of me on the ground he drew a cross and walked away." Aleksandr Solzhenitsyn said, "I knew that that was a message from God, and what I was about to do was wrong, and I settled back down." He said, "Little did I know that all over the world people were talking about me and in three days I would be a free man in Switzerland, in three days."

Wait on God. Don't be unwilling to wait. Humble yourselves under the mighty hand of God. In due time, He'll lift you up. When you don't understand, friend, don't get feverish. Don't you hurry God"

(Adrian Rogers, *When Nothings Seems to Make Sense,* Sermon # 2248, Love Worth Finding Ministries, Inc.).

Psalm of David

King Saul sought to take David's life for fifteen years. Even through this adversity, as David was running and hiding in caves, he kept his delight in the Lord. He was later rewarded by God to become king himself. David talks to us about 4-key concepts in Psalm 37:

I. Trust in the Lord.
II. Delight yourself in the Lord
III. Commit yourself to the Lord
IV. Rest in the Lord

I. Trust in the Lord

During challenging times in our life, we to try to figure out and understand things. God's word tells us to trust in Him with all our heart and lean not to own understanding, and He will direct our paths. As mentioned earlier, there is no way you can know God's mind; His ways are mysterious. In this chapter, David reminds us that the wicked and evildoers may be prosperous, and everything they do seems to go their way. However, the time is coming when God will cut off the wicked, and they shall be no more. Let us do what is right and do good in an evil world.

II. Delight Yourself in the Lord

We should start our day being joyful and happy. "This is the day the Lord has made; We will rejoice and be glad in it" (Psalm 118:24). David says we are to delight ourselves in the Lord. Even during the difficult times, we should be praising and delighting ourselves in the Lord not only when things are going well. We should be fortunate for the good times and for the not-so-good times.

There will be turmoil in our lives for no apparent reason; it just pops up out of nowhere. What can you do about it? You can worry day and night about it. You can have several sleepless nights. Or you can turn it over to Lord and let Him deal with it. You are less likely to be anxious when your heart, mind, and soul are with the Lord. "Be anxious for nothing", the Bible tells us, and give all your worries to God.

In 1 Peter 5:7, Peter tells us to cast our cares onto God. Since Peter was a fisherman before he became a disciple, he knows how to throw a net in the sea. To "cast" means to "throw" or "heave." Most people hang onto their cares or their worries instead of giving them to God. Anxiety is a killer, but it doesn't have to be. Heave your problems onto God; throw them away, and let God crush them.

Not often does one catch a fish on the first cast. But what does the fisherman do? He casts the line back out into the water. So, keep casting. Take delight in the Lord, and He will give you the desires of your heart. Here is what we say today, "God's got this." Believe this to be true and watch what God will do for you.

III. Commit Yourself to the Lord
Jesus tells us to pick up our cross and follow Him. Have you ever visualized Jesus carrying His cross after he was practically whipped to death? It was a struggle, but Jesus carried His cross to Calvary. We may also struggle to carry our crosses, but we must be "all in." We must commit ourselves to the Lord.

IV. Rest in the Lord
Patience is a learned virtue. God tells us to rest, to wait in Him, and He will bless us. "They that wait on the Lord shall be renewed with strength," the Bible tells us. God says, "Be still and know I am God."

Change is Inevitable.
Things in nature tend to follow the path of least resistance. We do not want to struggle. We want to take the easy route. Even though the simple path with the least resistance keeps us in a comfortable and less challenging place in our lives, ultimately, it becomes stale, and we're faced with changing the course.

We tend to avoid change. It is a risk that fills us with the fear of losing familiarity and makes us vulnerable by placing us in unknown territory. I was reluctant to give up being the person I worked so hard to become, although I really didn't like that person until the day, I picked up my cross and followed Jesus. Change can be challenging. However, we cannot live without changing any more than waking up in the morning without feeling the sun's warmth on our faces. It is a new day, and the sun continues to shine.

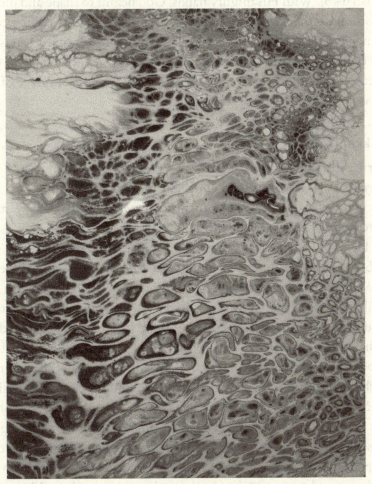

Psychedelic Wave

Change is inevitable—it happens whether we like it or not. Because of our sinful nature, we must change to be acceptable to God. We cannot change ourselves to be righteous with God, nor can we save ourselves. We need a mediator; we need a savior. We need Jesus Christ, who took on our sins and filth, and made us clean through His precious blood when He died on the cross. When we accepted Jesus Christ as our Lord and savior, we were changed forever and became righteous with God.

God's word tells us, "But now, O Lord, You are our Father; We are the clay, and You are the potter; And all we are the work of Your hand" (Isaiah 64:8). With His mighty hands, God begins to shape and mold us according to the way he designed for us to be. The Holy Spirit comes in and begins to clean our "spiritual house." The Holy Spirit bends here and twists there, squeezing out anything that is not acceptable to God. It refines us with love, joy, and peace to be in the perfect image of who He wants us to be—to be more like Jesus.

Wakeup Call

During difficult times, we should be praising God. *Why should we be grateful for the bad times?* God allows us to go through individual trials or circumstances in our lives to make a point. God is always up to something when a particular event sets us back.

He allows us to go through hardship even when we have done nothing wrong. It may seem unfair but read about Joseph in Genesis 39. When Joseph was sold as a slave at 17 years old and remained a slave until 30 years of age, he was not angry at God. Joseph was "calm as a cucumber," as the saying goes. The Bible informs us that, "God was with Him." There is an underlying reason why He allows us to go through trying times. He is testing our faith, but He is also trying to teach us something. If we are not paying attention, God will speak up.

Sometimes, God uses adversity to wake us up in the class of life. Life is an on-going learning process; at times, we are day-sleeping. We are somberly wandering around just living life, then boom! Some event happens to us, and we are in a mess. God may say, *"Hey, listen to me."* And we need to say, *"Okay God, you have my attention. What are you trying to tell me?"* We should understand that He is trying to do what is best for us, and not sulk in bitterness. Instead, we should be grateful that God has allowed these things to happen. Why? Read what James tells us: "My brethren, count it all joy when you fall into various trials, knowing that the testing of your faith produces patience" (James 1:2–3).

Difficult Times

We do not learn much when things are going well. For the most part, we take the good times for granted. It is during the difficult times when we learn valuable lessons. When we are following God's plan and come across hard times, it's God testing our faith. The point I am leading to is what may happen when we do not follow God's will as he has set for us.

Assuming we have not been following God's lead, we will have to face the consequences of our choices and go through difficult situations. These are the moments when we feel liking shouting, "Ugh"! We can become complacent and not call on God's counsel. He will bring us down to earth from the cloud we have been floating on to change our course of direction. The strange part about it is we begin to change during these challenging times. That's because we realize that God is bigger than any problem we may face. He allowed a particular event or situation to occur, but here is the fascinating part; He will bring us out of it too. He will not let us go alone; He is always by our side.

During these difficult times, we learn from Paul's affliction, when God said, "My grace is sufficient for you" (2 Corinthians 12:9). We know to become more dependent upon God. You may try to live your life apart from God, but eventually you will hit rock bottom. You soon realize that you cannot do anything without God's counsel. The moment you start trusting in God, your trials become easier to withstand. When the winds of life attempt to blow you over, God is there upholding you. Remember, during the tough and challenging times, we become mentally secure. Our Christian roots grow deeper

Difficult Times Changes Us

During the difficult times when nothing seems to go right, we pray more to God than ever before. We pray early in the morning, and we pray after the morning rush. We pray at lunch, dinner, and before we go to sleep. We diligently seek Him out daily and nightly through His Word so we can understand His ways. And before we realize it, we are in an intimate relationship with our Heavenly Father. Once we are proved to be faithful servants and that we would not deviate from God's plan He has designed for us, we begin to feel close to Him.

Our heart has been opened to see and understand God's will for us in our life. Our vision becomes clear to see His righteousness and truthfulness. Our walk with God becomes grounded with unwavering faith and unfaltering obedience. When we walk with courage and confidence during these testing times, we learn to be obedient to Him. Our motivation to be obedient to God is out of love and reverent fear of Him.

The Fear of the Lord

The Bible tells us that the beginning of knowledge is to fear the Lord (Proverbs 1:7). It's impossible to know God's ways without knowledge of Him. To gain that we must have a reverent fear of Him. King Solomon explains how we understand the fear of the Lord: "If you receive my words, and treasure my commands within you, So that you incline your ear to wisdom, and apply your heart to understanding; Yes, if you cry out for discernment, and lift your voice for understanding, If you seek her as silver, and search for her as for hidden treasures; Then you will understand the fear of the Lord, and find the knowledge of God. For the Lord gives wisdom; From His mouth come knowledge and understanding" (Proverbs 2:1–5).

We are to have a reverent fear of God by recognizing that He is sovereign. He is the Almighty, and is the Most High. He is the Creator and controller of all things. When we understand God's sovereignty and gain wisdom and knowledge, our whole demeanor changes out of respect for Him. We want to follow His will and behave according to His Word. We have the same fears and concerns a child demonstrates fear and care over their parents.

A child knows there will be repercussions if there is disobedience. That's the right kind of fear for a child to have. A well-nurtured child, with proper discipline understands that disobedience hurts the parents. They do not want to disobey their parents due to the love and respect they have for their parents. And this is how we should fear God too. He is not going to throw down a bolt of lightning on you if you are disobedient. However, not following His ways will hurt Him. My mom used to say, "This hurts me more than it hurts you." If you have children, you know what she meant. The Bible says we must fear the

Lord. We must have respect and reverence for Him and want to please Him in all our ways.

When we focus on God and have our eyes on Him, we remain obedient. When He says, "come," we follow. Ask for an understanding of God's will for your life and follow His plan he designed for you. We learn about God's will by reading His Word. Ask God to show you His will for your life. No good thing does God withhold from those who love Him. When God gives you His answer, follow it. He will not steer you down a path you cannot handle. He is always with you. Wherever God leads—go!

Learning from Elders

It astonishes me how some people can love every ounce of life—the good and bad times. They're the ones who express gratitude to God for everything. Not many people are genuinely grateful for what they have as those can be.

While visiting his wife in the hospital, I talked to an older gentleman, who expressed his blessings straight from the heart. He said he was a simple man and was not into material things. He told me that life was a precious gift. He went on to say that not every day in His life was perfect but only dwelled on the positive things. He said, "Get this, God gives us just enough to understand what He is doing. We do not know for sure what He has planned overall. But if you stick with Him long enough and follow His Word, you will be ahead of the game. If you do what He says, you will be rewarded in many ways. Most of what you get is right here", he said while pointing at his heart.

*God is like the sun; you cannot look
at it, but without it you cannot look at
anything else*—G.K. Chesterton

CHAPTER 7
Rain, Fear, and Fire

"He leads me beside the still waters. He restores my soul; He leads me in the paths of righteousness for His name's sake. Yea, though I walk through the valley of the shadow of death, I fear no evil; for You are with me; Your rod and Your staff, they comfort me"—Psalm 23: 2–4

Cracked Pot

A water bearer in India had two large pots. Each hung on one end of the pole he carried across the back of his neck. One of the pots had a crack in it. While the other pot was perfect and always delivered a full portion of water at the end of the long walk from the stream, the cracked pot arrived only half full. This went on for two years. The bearer delivered only one and a half pots of water to His master's house every day.

After two years of what it perceived as a bitter failure, the pot spoke to the water bearer. One day by the stream, it said, "I am ashamed of myself and I want to apologize to you." "Why?" asked the bearer, "What are you ashamed of?" "For the past two years, I have been able to deliver only half my load because this crack in my side causes water to leak. By the time, you make it all the way back to your master's house, you're left with only half. Because of my flaws you have to work without getting the full value of your efforts," the pot said.

The bearer said to the pot, "Did you notice that there were flowers only on your side of your path, but not on the other pot's side? That is because I knew about your flaw and took advantage of it. I planted flower seeds on your side of the path, and every day while we walk back from the stream, you've watered them for me. For two years I have been able to pick these beautiful flowers to decorate my master's table. If you were not just the way you are, he would not have such beauty to grace His house" (Anonymous author).

You Are Wonderfully Made

You may think, at times, that God blessed so many other people with the qualities you do not have. You may want to be better looking, more intelligent, and athletic, the list can go on. God knows all things. He knew you before you were born and set a plan for your life for His good pleasure. You may be living in your past, but God knows your future. He perfectly designed you the way he wanted for His glory. God does not seek out our perfections but instead uses our imperfections in His divine plan.

For many years as a teenager, I was trying to be like that other person. The well-liked guy in school. A guy who drove the new sports car. Or, the guy who all the girls went crazy over. What God taught me was that I was already person I wanted to be. So, be the person God created you to be. "But now, Lord, You are our Father; We are the clay, and You are the potter; and all we are the work of our hand" (Isaiah 64:8).

We all have something we are not good at doing. However, we also have talents and capabilities that others do not. Focus on the abilities that God gave you and serve the Lord wholeheartedly with joy. Walk with Him in bold steps of faith and confidence. Do it so that you may see His blessings and the rich rewards He has planned for you.

Flowers

A SUMMER RAIN

Heavenly Father, you are mighty to be praised. I give you all the honor and glory. I love you with my whole heart and come to you asking for your divine guidance.

You are the light that brightens my daily walk. I may stumble, but you always lift me. You tell me to be still and assure me that you are in control. Your Word says you will never leave nor forsake me. You are faithful to your promises.

You knew me before I was born, and say I am wonderfully made. You are a loving God, who stretches out His mighty hands with an abundance of love, grace, and mercy. You have given me peace. Father, your grace falls on me like summer rain. I am a plant that does not wither. I am tree rooted by the living waters. I shall not be moved.

Father, I ask that your holy Word spread across the world like a flaming fire. I pray for all people to hear the good news that Jesus Christ, your Son, who you sent to this world for the salvation of all humanity, is coming soon. In Him, they will be saved and live for eternity in your kingdom. Send the disciples of Christ with boldness and courage to spread the gospel to all who have ears to hear.

Father, give strength to the weak, comfort them and restore the joy of their salvation. Lift their weakened spirit and mend their broken hearts. Nothing is impossible with you. Promote health and wellness to those who are sick. You are the master physician, who can heal all things.

Teach me wisdom and give me discernment to understand and know that I am doing your will. I praise your holy name in the morning and all day long. I can do all things through you who gives me strength.

Father, I am forever grateful for the blessings you have given to my family and me. May the peace of Christ reign in my heart. Lead and direct my steps through the Holy Spirit to walk in righteousness and obedience to your Will. Guard my heart with your unfailing love. Keep me from temptation and deliver me from evil. Forgive me of my sins. In Jesus's holy name, I pray, Amen!

His Glory

"Now to Him who is able to keep you from stumbling, and to present you faultless before the presence of His glory with exceeding joy, to God our savior, Who alone is wise, be glory and majesty, dominion, and power, both now and forever. Amen" (Jude 1:24–25).

When I Stumble

"If I say, "My foot slips," Your mercy, O Lord, will hold me up. In the multitude of my anxieties within me, Your comforts delight my soul" (Psalm 94:18–19).

Rivers of Water

"He shall be like a tree planted by the rivers of water, that brings forth its fruit in its season, whose leaf also shall not wither; and whatever he does shall prosper" (Psalm 1:3).

Rooted in Faith

"As you therefore have received Christ Jesus the Lord, so walk in Him, rooted and built up in Him and established in the faith, as You have been taught, abounding in it with thanksgiving" (Colossians 2:6–7).

It Shall be Done

"If you abide in Me, and My words abide in you, you will ask what you desire, and it shall be done for you" (John 15:7).

The Love of God

"For I am persuaded that neither death nor life, nor angels nor principalities nor powers, nor things present nor things to come, nor height nor depth, nor any other created thing, shall be able to separate us from the love of God which is in Christ Jesus our Lord" (Romans 8:38–39).

God of Comfort

"Blessed be the God and Father of our Lord Jesus Christ, the Father of mercies and God of all comfort, who comforts us in all our tribulation, that we may be able to comfort those who are in any trouble, with the comfort with which we ourselves are comforted by God" (2 Corinthians 1:3–4).

The Holy Spirit

"However, when He, the Spirit of truth, has come, He will guide you into all truth; for He will not speak on His own authority, but whatever He hears He will speak; and He will tell you things to come" (John 16:13).

OPEN THE EYES OF MY HEART

Heavenly Father, I come to you today humbly proclaiming your majesty and holiness. You are an awesome God. There is none greater than you Lord; Your throne is forever and ever. I praise your holy name on bended knee, seeking your divine guidance.

Open the eyes of my heart, so I can see your ways and do your will. I need you; I am nothing without you. I have called out to you daily and have stretched my hands to you; You hear my cry and answer me.

Father, you know all things. You know my past when I walked back to you. Even so, Lord, you ran to me with loving arms and celebrated my return. You dry the wet of my eyes and restore my soul. Your love for me is more than I can imagine. I love you with my whole heart.

Cleanse the stain in my heart and paint it with your everlasting righteousness. Teach me to show kindness and lovingness to a world filled with hate. Your Word says that you pour love into hearts. Father, my heart is saturated with the blood of Christ.

Guide my steps to be more acceptable to you. Lead and direct my life to become more like Jesus's. I may fail you Lord, but you never fail me. Your love is everlasting. I may get upset, but you lift me. I may fall short, but you will never let go of me. I am convinced that no man can tell me otherwise. You are always beside me helping me with your righteous right hand. Thank you, Father. Let my countenance shine ever so brightly that people see your light in me.

Father, I pray that you will uplift the broken-hearted. Comfort and bless them with your unfailing love. Promote wellness to those who are sick. Heal their bodies with your mighty hands. Give to those who fervently seek you. Show abundant blessings to all your children.

I pray that you will protect us from the evilness and wickedness in this world. Deliver us from temptation. Lead Your disciples to spread the gospel of Jesus Christ to all who accept and believe in Him. Give faith to nonbelievers and open their hearts that you wish no one to perish but live eternally in your kingdom.

Father, you are worthy of all praise and glory. You give me the courage to withstand any storm. I can do all things through you. I am forever grateful for the blessings you have given to my family and me. Continue to bless us, Lord. Guard and comfort my heart with your never-ending love. Thank you, Father, for hearing my prayer. In the mighty name of Jesus, I pray. Amen.

Filled with the Spirit

When you accept Jesus into your life, the Holy Spirit comes in and takes the unacceptable things within your heart and gets rid of them, and fills your heart with love, joy, and peace. When the Holy Spirit dwells in your heart, He moves into your life, removes piece by piece of the old you, and changes the new you, bit by bit. Be filled with the spirit.

The Holy Temple

"Do you not know that your body is the temple of the Holy Spirit who is in you, whom you have from God, and you are not your own" (1 Corinthians 6:19)?

All That I Do

"And whatever you do in word or deed, do all in the name of the Lord Jesus, giving thanks to God the Father through Him" (Colossians 3:17).

THE FIRE THAT WARMS MY HEART

Heavenly Father, you are the Almighty God; you are the God of all things. I fall to my knees, humbly proclaiming your holiness. Today is the day that you have made, and I will rejoice and be glad in it.

Father, I search deep into your Word to know you and to do your will. Your Word says to be strong and courageous. Your Word tells me that you will teach me the way with your eyes on me; Give me wisdom and understanding of your ways. You are the fire that warms my heart and the light that directs my steps.

I am a sinner, and I need you. I cast all my cares upon you because you care for me. You are my strength and shield. My heart trusts in you. You crush my enemies underneath my feet, and nothing formed against me shall stand.

Father, you know the depths of my heart. You knew me before I was born. You know my past, present, and future. When I call out your name, you are already there with arms wide open. Nothing is greater than the unconditional love you have for me.

By your grace, you sent your only Son to shine His precious light on the world for salvation, that anyone who accepts and confesses that Jesus Christ is Lord and savior would be saved. When I ask for you to take this thorn from my side, you say, your grace is enough. It pours down like rain from the heavens. You cleanse me from all unrighteousness.

Father, you demonstrated your power by raising Christ from the dead; nothing is impossible to you. Resurrect the hearts of those who are going through trials. Show your healing power to promote health and wellness to those who are sick. Show abundant blessings to those who love you.

I ask that you give faith to nonbelievers, for you wish that no one should perish. Open their hearts to hear the truth of your Word. Give them the faith to believe in your Son. Teach me to love and pray for my enemies and those who persecute and hate me for Jesus's namesake. Teach me, Lord, to forgive others as you have done unto me. Thank you for the blessings you have given to my family and me. Guard and protect me from evil and deliver me from temptation. Forgive me of my sins. In Jesus's name, I pray. Amen.

The God of Hope

"Now may the God of hope fill you with all joy and peace in believing, that you may abound in hope by the power of the Holy Spirit" (Romans 15:13).

Rejoice and be Glad

"This is the day the Lord has made, We will rejoice and be glad in it" (Psalm 118:24).

Blessed are Those

"Blessed are the undefiled in the way, who walk in the law of the Lord! Blessed are those who keep His testimonies, who seek Him with the whole heart! They also do no iniquity; They walk in His ways" (Psalm 119:1–3).

Fear of God

"You shall walk after the Lord your God and fear Him and keep His commandments and obey His voice; you shall serve Him and hold fast to Him" (Deuteronomy 13:4).

Wisdom and Knowledge

"The fear of the Lord is the beginning of wisdom, and the knowledge of the Holy One is understanding" (Proverbs 9:10).

He is a Shield

"He is a shield to all who trust in Him" (Psalm 18:30).

The Lord Knows

"O Lord, You have searched me and known me. You know my sitting down and my rising up; You understand my thought afar off. You comprehend my path and my lying down, and are acquainted with all my ways" (Psalm 139: 1–3).

Confess with Your Mouth

"That if you confess with your mouth the Lord Jesus and believe in your heart that God has raised Him from the dead, you will be saved" (Romans 10:9).

Grant me, O Lord my God, a mind to know you, a heart to seek you, wisdom to find you, conduct pleasing to you, faithful perseverance in waiting for you, and a hope of finally embracing you. Amen—Thomas Aquinas

CHAPTER 8
Be Still

"Meditate within your heart on your bed and be still. Selah. Offer the sacrifices of righteousness and put your trust in the Lord"—Psalm 4:4–5

Do Not Sin

It is normal to be frustrated at times, especially in this world today. God's word tells us that it is okay to show our anger, but do not sin (Psalm 4:4). Jesus got angry with the Jewish people in the temple because they were corrupting God's house. He had a reason to be angry. The Jewish people had turned God's temple from a place of prayer into "a den of thieves" (Matthew 21:13).

As Christians, we are to demonstrate godly behavior. We are to show kindness and to love one another. We are to forgive those who do us wrong. Jesus told us to forgive seventy times seven (Matthew 18:22). Now, that does not mean you stop forgiving your brother at 490. If you must forgive your brother a hundred thousand times, forgive as the Lord has forgiven you.

When you get upset or angry about something, close your eyes, take a few deep breaths, and concentrate on your breathing. It is challenging to remain in a bothered state of mind while exercising this mind-clearing technique. It is hard to stay frustrated when you are praising and worshipping God in prayer.

If you add fuel to an already flaming fire, the fire only becomes immense. Stop! Reflect on what God would have you do. Ask God to help you with the situation that is causing your anger. If you are wrong about a specific matter, the Holy Spirit within you will lead you straight. If you are right about whatever is causing your anger, take it to the Lord in prayer. Or, take it to the church leaders, but see that you do not sin. Always put your trust in the Lord.

Led by the Spirit

A sinful nature is hostile toward God since it does not abide by His laws. Now, when believing and accepting Jesus Christ saves us from separation from God, we are still prone to sin. It does not mean we do not have a sinful nature; we were born into it. Nevertheless, as believers, we are in a Spirit-frame of mind, even when we sin against God. Thus, we are still saved.

We are to avoid worldly or carnal things, which are against God. We are to be led by the Spirit and not of the flesh. "For if you live according to the flesh you will die; but if by the Spirit you put to death the deeds of the body, you will live. For as many as are led by the Spirit of God, these are sons of God" (Romans 8: 13–14).

SPIRIT OF PEACE

Dear Father, thank you for your blessings you have given to me. You are an awesome God. I worship and praise your holy name. I come to you today with a humble and open heart seeking your divine instruction and wisdom.

Lead me in this world free from anger. Take the spirit of anger and replace it with the spirit of peace. Father, you are the author of peace, the God of comfort and mercy. Be merciful to me and mold my heart to be more like your precious Son's. Free me from anything that is not acceptable to you. I desire to live according to your will. Teach me your good ways.

Teach me to love and to show compassion as you have given love and compassion to me. Teach me to forgive as you have done for me. Open my heart and sustain it with your holy Word.

I stand at the foot of the cross and follow my Lord and savior, Jesus Christ. Change me to be more like Him. Direct my steps to walk on the narrow path, which leads to your holy kingdom. Keep evil and wickedness far from my family and me. Shield and protect us under the shadow of your wings.

Show healing to the sick and comfort the hearts of the broken-hearted. Pour out your blessings to all who love you wholeheartedly. Show abundant blessings to us. Forgive me of my sins. In Jesus's name, I pray. Amen.

YOUR TENDER MERCIES

Heavenly Father, you are the only true living God. I praise, magnify, and honor you with all my heart, mind, and soul. I humble myself before you, Lord seeking your wisdom.

Please give me the strength to stand against the evil in this world and those against you. Protect my family and me from wickedness. You are all-powerful, who can do all things. Heal my heart. Lift my spirit with your tender mercies and loving-kindness.

Father, I pray for this world that you would comfort those who are persecuted and killed in the name of Jesus. Restore the joy of our salvation to all who love you across the world. Through your Son, we have an inheritance waiting for us in your kingdom.

Lord, give faith to those who do not know your Son. Give them faith to believe that you wish no one to perish but come to you in repentance and follow Christ. Father teach me how to follow your will. Lead and direct my steps through the Holy Spirit to walk in your holy ways. Show abundant blessings to my family and me. Forgive me of my sins. In Jesus's name, I pray. Amen.

If you do not know Jesus as your personal savior, right now is the time to give your life to Him. Ask Jesus to come into your heart and follow Him. May the God of glory bless and comfort you in Christ Jesus! Say this prayer: "Dear Jesus, I am a sinner. I believe you are the Son of God who died on the cross and rose on the third day. I ask that you come into my heart and take my burden. Forgive me of all my sins. In your holy name, I pray. Amen".

My friend, if you said this prayer for the first time, the Bible says, you are saved. You have been accepted into the royal family of the kingdom of God. And all God's people say—Amen!

Confess with your Mouth

"That if you confess with your mouth the Lord Jesus and believe in your heart that God has raised Him from the dead, you will be saved" (Romans 10:9).

Love the Lord

"You shall love the Lord your God with all your heart, with all your soul, and with all your mind" (Matthew 22:37).

Have Mercy

"Have mercy upon me, O God, according to Your loving kindness; according to the multitude of Your tender mercies, blot out my transgressions" (Psalm 51:1).

Wait Upon the Lord

"But those who wait upon the Lord shall renew their strength; they shall mount up with wings like eagles, they shall run and not be weary, they shall walk and not faint" (Isaiah 40:31).

God's Timing

Sometimes, God does not answer our prayer right away because the timing is not right, or God has something else planned that will be better for us. We are His children, and children do not understand the concept of time:

"Are we there yet"? The child asks.

"No, two more hours," says the dad.

Five minutes later, the child asks, "Are we there yet"?

Children can be a bundle of joy, and we can learn a lot from them. When we ask God about the answer to our prayer, He says, "Be still." We ask, "why"? God says, "Because I am God." In God's eyes, we adults are children to Him. However, we still ask God why. We get an understanding of God's time clock when we are close to Him. "Be still before the Lord and wait patiently for Him" (Psalm 37:7 NIV).

We begin to understand His timetable, not that we will know it completely when we have an unwavering trust in Him and are patient with Him. As we grow in Him, we begin to ask, *"What do you want me to do God"*?

When God does not answer your prayers as soon as you would like, trust in Him that He will answer your prayer. Place all your trust upon Him in all your ways. Be patient with faith, knowing that God will respond to you. Through trust and patience, He is preparing you for an abundance of rewards and success. He is strengthening your Christian roots to enable you to withstand any storm that life may bring. Trust in Him always. And thank God for everything.

Faithful Servant

A visiting tourist asked a gardener of a beautiful and well-kept mansion,

"How long have you been caretaker here?" The tourist asked the gardener.

"I've been here twenty years."

"And during that time, how often has the owner of the property been in residence?"

The gardener smiled. "He has been here only four times."

"And to think", the visitor exclaimed, "all these years you've kept this house and garden in such superb condition. You tend them as if you expect Him to come tomorrow."

"Oh no", replied the gardener, "I look after them as if I expected Him to come today." [1]

"Blessed is that servant whom His master, when he comes, will find so doing" (Matthew 24:46). Jesus wants us to be working as faithful servants until His return. Jesus said, "Surely I am coming quickly" (Revelation 22:20). Praise God the Father in heaven for our Blessed Hope in Jesus Christ, our Lord. Amen and amen!

Nothing tends more to cement the hearts of Christians than praying together. Never do they love one another so well as when they witness the outpouring of each other's hearts in prayer—Charles Finney

CHAPTER 9
Short Prayers

"For the eyes of the Lord are on the righteous, and His ears are open to their prayers"—1 Peter 3:11.

WITHSTAND THE STORM

Heavenly Father, thank you for your love, grace, and mercy. Thank you, Lord, for my blessings. You are an awesome God, who can do all things. Give me strength to withstand the storms of this world and strengthen my faith to trust and obey.

Show blessings to my family and me. Keep evil and wickedness from us Lord and protect us with Your Holy hands. Teach me wisdom and give me discernment to understand your will for my life. Thank you, God, for loving me and hearing my prayer. Forgive me of my sins. In the name of Jesus, amen!

I AM A SINNER

Dear Jesus, I am a sinner. I have said and done things in my life that I am not proud of. Please cleanse me and become the Lord of my life. Your Word says that if I ask for forgiveness, you are faithful and just to forgive me and to cleanse me from all unrighteousness.

I believe you are the Son of the living God and that you died for my sins on the cross. I also believe that you were raised from the dead and now sit at the right hand of God the Father. I believe this with all my heart and from this day forward, I want to live for you. Forgive me of my sins. In your name, I pray. Amen.

DAILY GUIDANCE

Heavenly Father, thank you for the blessings you have given to my family and me. You are the only true living God. Nothing compares to you. I come to you with a humble heart seeking your divine guidance.

Father, you are the lamp to my feet. I need your guidance to get me through this day. Lift my spirit and hold me with your mighty hands. You are my rock and fortress. I need you daily. Guard and protect me from the wickedness and evil in this world. Shield me under the shadow of your mighty wings.

Lead me to be the person you want me to be. Give me direction to walk in your ways. Teach me your wisdom and knowledge. Teach me how to discern your voice when you give me counsel. Guide me to stay on the path of righteousness through the Holy Spirit. Guard my heart with the warmth of your comforting love. Forgive me of my sins. In Jesus's name, I pray. Amen.

MORNING PRAYER

Dear Father, thank you for another day to praise and worship your holy name. You are an awesome God; You can do all things. Lead my feet to walk in obedience to do your will for my life. Open my eyes to see your great works. Open my mouth to speak truthfulness and righteousness. Open my heart to extend love and kindness to all your creation. Guard and comfort me throughout the day. Lift me up with the strength of your mighty hands. Let all that I do today be acceptable to you. Forgive me of my sins. In the mighty name of Jesus, I pray. Amen.

RESTORE MY MARRIAGE

Father God, there is none like you. I come to you with a broken heart seeking your love and healing. Hear my prayer. I ask that you restore my marriage with my husband. Take away His desire to drink. Take away the things that makes him angry. Help him on his job and fill his heart with peace. We need you father to heal our family. Show blessing and healing to us. Send us the means, Father, to pay our bills and rent. Keep our kids safe and keep them healthy. Forgive us of our sins. In Jesus name, amen.

COMMIT TO JESUS

Dear Jesus, thank You for the sacrifice of dying on the cross for my sins. I open the door of my heart for you to come in and change my life. I accept and believe you are my Lord and savior. I commit my life to you and will pick up my cross daily and follow you. Mold and reshape my life to be the person you want me to be. Forgive me of all my sins. In your name I pray. Amen.

CENTER OF MY LIFE

Dear Lord Jesus, I am forever grateful for your sacrifice for my sins. I desire to walk in Christ as the center of my life. Teach me to love as you love. Teach me to forgive others as you have forgiven me. Come into my heart and fill it with your kindness, goodness, and truthfulness.

Direct my paths to walk obeying our Father in heaven as you have shown your obedience to Him. Teach to me serve and obey without grumbling or complaining, but to do all things justly and honestly from the heart.

Deliver me from temptation and from evil. Show blessings in all that I do. Secure my heart with your never-ending love. Forgive me of my sins. In Your name I pray, Amen.

PURGE MY HEART

Dear gracious, Heavenly Father, I praise your holy name forevermore. You are a sovereign God who deserves all the glory, power, and honor. I come to you with a humble heart seeking your divine guidance.

I serve You with all my heart and strive daily to walk in your ways. Teach me wisdom and give me knowledge to follow your will in my life. Keep my mind on pure and just thoughts; keep me far from evil and wickedness.

Forgive me of my sins in Jesus's name. Purge my heart from any unrighteousness and fill it with your never-ending love, grace, and mercy. Thank you for the blessings that you have given to me. Lead me through the Holy Spirit to follow your ways. Direct me Father to be holy as you are holy. Let the peace of Christ remain in my heart in all that I do. In Jesus's name, I pray. Amen.

A SINNER'S CRY

Dear Lord, I have not followed you or believed all your ways. I have done things according to what I wanted to do, and I realize I was wrong. My life is in such a mess, I have ruined relationships with my family and friends.

I have sinned and done things regardless of if they were wrong in your eyes; I am sorry. I need help; I cannot do this any longer by myself. I have cried and cried so many tears, and they seem to keep falling with no end in sight. Help me Lord to see the light. Help me to change my ways.

I need you Lord. I believe that Jesus Christ was born from a virgin, died on the cross, rose on the third day, and ascended to heaven to be at Your right-hand side. I accept Jesus Christ as my Lord and savior. Forgive me Lord; take all my sins and wash them away. In Jesus's name I pray. Amen.

BLESS OUR COUNTRY

Heavenly Father, thank you for our blessings. Thank you for your grace and mercy that you have shown to us. You are an awesome God. There is none like you. We praise your holy name and love you with all our heart.

Bless our country and our military throughout the world. Give strength to our soldiers and servicemen, guard and protect them under the shadow of your wings. Bring them home soon to the loving embrace of their families.

Thank you, Father, for sending our Lord Jesus Christ to die on the cross for our sins. Place your healing hand upon our family and show blessings to us. Heal and comfort those who need you close to them. Guide our steps and actions through the Holy Spirit and lead us to always seek to do your will. Deliver us from temptation and from evil. Comfort our hearts with your unfailing love, grace, and mercy. Forgive us of our sins. In Jesus's name we pray. Amen.

NO ONE COMPARES TO YOU

Dear Father, I love you with my whole heart. You are an awesome God; You can do all things. Thank you for being merciful to me. Grant me wisdom to understand your ways.

Guide my steps to walk in obedience to your will in my life. Show abundant blessings to me and show me the work of your lovingkindness. No one compares to you Father; your kingdom is forever and ever; I praise you all day long.

You make me confident to withstand any storm that comes my way. Thank you for loving me. Deliver me from temptation and from evil and wickedness. Thank you, Father, for hearing and answering my prayer. Guard my heart with your never-ending love. Forgive me of my sins. In Jesus's holy name I pray. Amen!

A Prayer of Moses
"I pray, if I have found grace in Your sight, show me now Your way, that I may know You and that I may find grace in Your sight"(Exodus 33:13).

Be Confident in the Lord
"Being confident of this very thing, that He who has begun a good work in you will complete it until the day of Jesus Christ" (Philippians 1:6).

YOUR KINGDOM IS FOREVER

Heavenly Father, you are the Most High who deserves all the glory, praise, and honor. Your kingdom is forever and ever. Open the eyes of my heart to see your goodness and righteousness. Lead my life with your ever-lasting brightness to shine ever so brightly that others may see your good works in me.

Grant me wisdom to understand your perfect ways. Give me discernment to hear your voice. Fill my heart with your unfailing love. Lead and direct my steps through the Holy Spirit to do your will. Give me insight to follow your plan you set for me, that I may be acceptable to you.

Father, forgive me of my transgressions. Keep evil from my family and me. Show abundant blessings to us. Thank you, Father, for your grace, love, and mercy. All this I ask in Jesus's holy name. Amen.

The Perfect Way
"As for God, His way is perfect; The word of the Lord is proven; He is a shield to all who trust in Him" (Psalm 18:30).

JOB INTERVIEW

Heavenly Father, thank you for my blessings. You are all-Powerful. You can do all things. Your word tells me to be anxious for nothing, but to pray and you will guide me.

Father, you know what is best for me. A good Father does what is best for His children. I have confidence in you Lord. I can do all things through You. I place my future into your hands and live to do your will.

Father, I ask that you calm my soul from unwanted fears and worry. Lead and direct my actions during my job interview with courage and boldness that I have nothing to fear for you are with me. If it is your will, give me this job that I may serve you. Show me your never-ending love, grace, and mercy. Thank you, Father, for hearing my prayer. Forgive me of my sins. In Jesus's name, I pray. Amen.

The Children of God

"Behold what manner of love the Father has bestowed on us, that we should be called children of God! Therefore the world does not know us, because it did not know Him. Beloved, now we are children of God; and it has not yet been revealed what we shall be, but we know that when He is revealed, we shall be like Him, for we shall see Him as He is. And everyone who has this hope in Him purifies Himself, just as He is pure" (1 John 3:1–3).

Eyes of the Lord

"For the eyes of the Lord are on the righteous, and His ears are open to their prayers; But the face of the Lord is against those who do evil" (1 Peter 3:11–12).

The Most High

"I will praise the Lord according to His righteousness, and will sing praise to the name of the Lord Most High" (Psalm 7:17).

Love in Deed and Truth

"Let us not love in word or in tongue, but in deed and in truth. And by this we know that we are of the truth … And this is His commandment: that we should believe on the name of His Son Jesus Christ and love one another" (1 John 3:18-19,23).

Let Your Light Shine

"Let your light so shine before men, that they may see your good works and glorify your Father in heaven" (Matthew 5:16).

The Value of Wisdom

"If you receive my words, and treasure my commands within you, So that you incline your ear to wisdom, and apply your heart to understanding; Yes, if you cry out for discernment, and lift your voice for understanding, If you seek her as silver, and search for her as for hidden treasures; Then you will understand the fear of the Lord, and find the knowledge of God. For the Lord gives wisdom; From His mouth come knowledge and understanding" (Proverbs 2:1–5).

STRENGTHEN MY FAMILY

Dear Heavenly Father, you are the Most High. There is none like you. We worship and praise your holy name. Your Word tells us to cast all our care upon you because you care for us.

Thank you, Father, for your unconditional love. Father take away any strongholds that may bring down my family. Renounce any spirit of fear, anger, or sorrow in the mighty name of Jesus. Keep us from procrastination and stagnation. Let us be the body of Christ that serves for your glory. Let us reach toward the prize for your high calling in Christ Jesus.

Father, guard and comfort us with the warmth of your never-ending love, grace, and mercy. Tug at the hearts of my family and draw them near to you with your loving and generous heart. You know our needs, Father. Rain down your blessings from heaven to ensure financial stability. Let peace reign in our hearts in all that we do. Forgive us of our sins. In Jesus's precious name, we pray. Amen!

FINDING THE RIGHT JOB

Dear Father, you are an awesome God. You are the Creator of all things. I am in awe of Your marvelous works. Father, You know my heart and want what is best for me. There is not a day that goes by that you do not have your eye upon me. When I get anxious, you tell me to be still and know that you are my God. You are always with me even during the trying times. You uphold me with your tender mercies with the righteousness of your right hand. You are my rock and shield. I have nothing to fear.

Father, show your abundant grace from heaven and provide financial stability for my family. Find the right job for me Lord so that I can support my family. Show blessings to my family and me. You are a great God. You are a generous God, who wants to give to those who love you with their whole heart. I am forever grateful for the blessings you have given to my family and me. Continue to bless us. Forgive me of my sins. I ask in the name of Jesus. Amen.

DIVINE PROTECTION

Heavenly Father, there is not a day that goes by that I do not praise your holy name. You are awesome. I come to you today with an open heart seeking your guidance and protection.

Guide my steps to walk in your holy ways. Let me be acceptable to show your good works in me. I seek your divine protection for my family and me. Guard us under the shadow of your mighty wings. Keep me far from temptation and deliver from the wiles of the devil. Comfort my heart with the peace of Christ that I have no fear or worries for you are always with me. Rain down your heavenly blessings on me from your warm and generous heart.

I am forever grateful for the blessings you have given to my family and me. Continue to bless us Lord with the abundance of your love, grace, and mercy. I praise your name in the morning. I praise your holy name all day long. You give me strength when I am weak; You calm my soul. I love you with all my heart. Let all that I do be done in the name of our Lord Jesus Christ. Forgive me of my sins. Thank you, Father, for hearing my prayer. In Jesus's name. Amen.

THE WARMTH OF YOUR LOVE

Dear Father, I come to you requesting your divine guidance in my life. You are my rock and shield. I need your strength. Your Word says that in my weakest moments, I am strong in you. You give the endurance to handle all things. Any challenge that comes into my life, I can handle through you who give strength and help me.

Lift my spirit. Calm my soul with the warmth of your love. Direct my steps to walk in the Holy Spirit full of love, joy, and peace. Uplift my spiritual life to think of godly things and not worldly things. Keep me from temptation. Keep me far from evil and wickedness but surround me with your goodness and with your light. Let the fire in my heart be lit to shine upon all to see your good works in me. I love you wholeheartedly, and I want to be pleasing to you. Thank you, Father, for hearing my prayer. Forgive me of my sins. In the name of Jesus, I pray. Amen!

HEALING

Heavenly Father, you are the Most High who can do all things. Nothing compares to you. I worship and praise your holy name and love you with all my heart. I come to today for you supernatural and divine healing.

Father, your word says that the prayer of faith will save the sick, and you will raise me up. You always hold true to your Word. Your promises are true. I trust in you in all that I do.

I place my body over to you as a living sacrifice Lord. You are my Creator, and you can heal all things. Your Word says to worry about nothing but to ask in prayer with thanksgiving that you will guard my heart in Christ Jesus. Thank you, Father, for never-ending love you have for me.

Show your miraculous healing power and heal my illness. Take away anything within me that causes harm to my body in Jesus's name. You are the master physician; nothing is impossible to you. Your word tells me that you will keep me in perfect peace whose mind is on you. I seek an intimate relationship with You. I want to know your good ways. I praise your holy name all day long. I am nothing without you in my life. Thank you, Father, for your grace that you have given so freely.

I know from the depths of my heart that you hear my prayer, and you will answer me according to your righteousness. Guard and comfort my heart with the peace of Christ. Keep evil far from me and deliver me from temptation. In the name of Jesus, I pray. Amen!

FOLLOW GOD'S LEAD

Heavenly Father, you and you alone are the only true living God, the Creator of all things. I am in awe of your marvelous wonders. I praise your holy name and come to you with a humble heart seeking your divine counsel.

Teach me to walk in your ways. Guide my steps and actions to always follow your lead in all that I do. Instruct me to make wise decisions that seek your will in my life. Let me hear your voice when you give me advice.

Show abundant blessings to my family and me. Secure me with the warmth of your unfailing love. I may fail you Lord, but you never let me down. You are always helping me with your righteous right hand. Through the blood of Jesus Christ, I belong to you.

Thank you for your never-ending love, grace, and mercy that you have bestowed upon me. Thank you, Father, for hearing my prayer. Guard, protect, and comfort me from temptation and from the evil of this world under the shadow of your mighty wings. Forgive me of all my sins. In the precious name of Jesus Christ, my Lord, I pray. Amen.

The good news is there is nothing we can do that is bad enough to keep us out of heaven; the bad news is there is nothing we can do good enough to get us into heaven—Zig Ziglar

CHAPTER 10
Our Heavenly Father

"Our Father in heaven, Hallowed be Your name, Your kingdom come. Your will be done on earth as it is in heaven. Give us this day our daily bread. And forgive us of our debts, as we forgive our debtors. And do not lead us into temptation, But deliver us from the Evil one. For Yours is the kingdom and the power and the glory forever. Amen"—Matthew 6:9–13

OUR FATHER IN HEAVEN

Our Father in heaven, hallowed be your name. You are good all the time. You are a gracious God. You are a loving God. You are all-powerful. Nothing compares to you. We come to you today with a humble and open heart to feel your presence with us.

Father, we could search the world over and never find a truer love than you. You are love, and we love you wholeheartedly. There is not a day that goes by that we do not praise your good name. Thank you for your unconditional love for us.

When we call out your name, you are already there. You are always with us. We have no fear of man or evil for You give us courage and strength. During trouble, you calm our hearts and restore our souls. When we worry, you tell us to be still and to know you have our back. You are always helping us with your righteous right hand.

Grant us the wisdom to understand your ways. Guide our steps to walk in faith with obedience to do your will. Open our hearts to love as you love. Extend our hands to show mercy as you show mercy. Father our sins may reach the tip of Mount Sinai. But your grace extends to the heavens, showering down on us like precious rain, washing away any unrighteousness. Thank you, Father, for your never-ending grace. Mold and reshape us to resemble the person we have always desired to be, and to be more like your precious Son.

Let the light of Christ in us spread like a wildfire proclaiming the good news. That our Lord and savior, Jesus Christ, is coming to redeem His church. All that believe in and accept Him shall have eternal life.

Father, your Word tells us that blessed is he who comes in the name of the Lord. We proclaim your holy name for all ears to hear. You are the Almighty God and Jesus Christ is the King of Kings and the Lord of Lords. Nothing can separate us from the love you have for us.

Bless the broken-hearted, comfort them with your unfailing love. Heal the sick with your mighty hands. Show blessings to all those who pour out their heart to you. Father forgive us of our trespasses as we forgive others. Shield and protect us from evil and wickedness. Teach us to love and pray for our enemies. Guard and protect our hearts with your love, grace, and mercy. Lead and direct our steps through the Holy Spirit to walk in your ways. Thank you for our blessings and may the peace of Christ reign in our hearts always. In Jesus's holy name we pray. Amen.

God is Love

At times, it is difficult to express love for people who dislike us or hate us. It may not be an easy step, but we must put one leg out in front of the other. Displaying love and kindness cools their hatred and confuses the enemy. God wants us to show love to all people. John writes to us, "Beloved, let us love one another, for love is of God; and everyone who loves is born of God and knows God" (1 John 4:7). Throughout the Bible, He teaches us stewardship. For God to bless us, we must bless others. Let the peace of Christ rule in your heart, and whatever you do, do it in the name of Jesus.

Loved by My Father

"He who has My commandments and keeps them, it is he who loves Me. And he who loves Me will be loved by My Father, and I will love him and manifest Myself to him" (John 14:21).

Blessed is He

"Blessed is he who comes in the name of the Lord" (Psalm 118:26).

God heals

"For I will restore health to you and heal you of your wounds, says the Lord" (Jeremiah 30:17).

SHORT GROUP PRAYER

Heavenly Father, we thank you for another day you have created. You are worthy of all honor, praise, and glory. We come to you humbly with fervent reverence proclaiming your majesty for your kingdom is forever and ever.

Keep our minds on godly things and not on worldly things. Lead and direct our steps and actions to be more like Jesus. Let our light shine onto all people to see your good works in us. Guard our hearts with the warmth of your unfailing love. Spread goodness, kindness, and truthfulness all around us in all that we do.

Heal us from internal and external wounds. Repair our hearts and fill it with your comforting love, grace, and mercy. Thank you for your unconditional love for us. Forgive us of our transgressions. In Jesus's name, we pray. Amen.

Do Something

Once upon a time, a very strong woodcutter asked for a job in a timber merchant, and he got it. The pay was good, and so were the work conditions. For those reasons, the woodcutter was determined to do his best. His boss gave him an axe and showed him the area where he was supposed to work. On the first day, the woodcutter brought in 18 trees.

"Congratulations," the boss said. "Go on your way!"

Very motivated by the boss's words, the woodcutter tried harder the next day, but he could only bring in 15 trees. The third day he tried even harder, but he could only bring in 10 trees. Day after day he was bringing less and less trees.

"I must be losing my strength," the woodcutter thought. He went to the boss and apologized, saying that he could not understand what was going on.

"When was the last time you sharpened your axe?" the boss asked.

"Sharpen? I had no time to sharpen my axe. I have been very busy trying to cut trees[1]."

Life can be busy. However, we should not be so occupied that we neglect to sharpen our "spiritual axe" otherwise we become spiritually dull. When we say, "I'll try to pray more", or "I'll try to read the Bible more", we are only committing ourselves half-way. If you say, "I'll try" it does not lock you into doing something. Your friend may say, "I thought you said you were coming to the company dinner." Your reply would be, I said, *"I'd try to come"*. Do you see my point? You did not *try* to get out of bed this morning; you did something to get out of bed. You did not *try* to brush your teeth or eat breakfast. *Trying* and *doing* are two different things.

Doers of the Word

"But be doers of the word, and not hearers only, deceiving yourselves. For if anyone is a hearer of the word and not a doer, he is like a man observing his natural face in a mirror, for he observes himself, goes away, and immediately forgets what kind of man he was"(James 1:22–24).

Sharpening your spiritual life is being close to God. It is being in God's house with fellow Christians. It is getting to know Him by prayer and by reading His word. You may tell yourself that you will try to pray more. When you tell that to yourself, it is not a commitment. Tell yourself that you *will* pray more. Stop *trying* to do something, and let God do something *in* you. Trust in Him always, be obedient to Him, and you will see His abundant blessings. You must not become so busy in life that you do not invest the time to spend with the Lord—make time!

CREATOR OF ALL THINGS

Heavenly Father, you are the Creator of all things. You are good all the time. We worship and praise your holy sovereign name and love you with our whole hearts. We express our thankfulness and gratefulness to you.

During the storm, you are always watching over us. As the birds of the air find a nest, you give us shelter because you hold us dear to your heart. There is nothing you withhold from your children. You are a loving God full of compassion, grace, and mercy.

We seek you in dark moments where all appears to fade from memory. But you, God, are all-knowing have a divine plan for each of us. You care for us like we are your precious treasures. Your Word tells us that you are always with us that you would never forsake us. You hold true to your promises, God. Thank you for loving us. There is not a greater love in this world other than you.

You knew each one of us before we were born, watched us grow, and say we are wonderfully made. You dry the tear in our eye and give us peace. You have created a plan for our life, and soon you will deliver your promises. We all claim your mighty promises to us Father. Give us patience when we are anxious. Calm our souls when we are upset. There is not a day that goes by that we do not wish to be in your presence.

You are our Heavenly Father who loves us more than we can ever imagine. You want what is best for us and will not settle for anything but the best. Take any doubt or sorrow from our heart and fill it your never-ending, unwavering love. Walk with us daily so we may live in righteousness and truthfulness.

Teach us Lord to live in your ways. Teach us to always be kind and how to love the people we do not like. Mold our lives to be more like Jesus's. Fill our hearts with love, grace, and mercy. Show abundant blessings to us Father. Let your precious grace rain down on us.

Thank You, Father, for all that you have given to us. Shield us under the shadow of your wings. Protect us from evil and deliver us from temptation. We ask for the forgiveness of our sins. In Jesus's holy name we pray, Amen.

The Word of God is edge all over. It is alive in every part, and in every part keen to cut the conscience and wound the heart. Depend on it: not a verse in the Bible is superfluous or a chapter that is useless—Charles Spurgeon

CHAPTER 11
The Word of God

"For the word of God is living and powerful, and sharper than any two-edged sword, piercing even to the division of soul and spirit, and of joints and marrow, and is a discerner of the thoughts and intents of the heart"—Hebrews 4:12

TABLET OF MY HEART

Dear, gracious, Heavenly Father, you are an awesome God worthy of all glory, honor, and power. I praise and worship your Holy name and love you with my whole heart. Thank you, Father, for your divine guidance.

You are the light that brightens my path. Your Word is my map that directs my steps. You guide me all day long. Lead and direct my steps through the Holy Spirit to do your will.

Thank you for your Son who you gave to the world for the forgiveness of sins and for eternal salvation. My sins may reach the highest mountain on earth, but your grace extends to the heavens. You blot out all my transgressions through the blood of Jesus Christ.

Write your Word on the tablet of my heart, and let your Son shine ever so brightly in my life to show your everlasting love and kindness to others. Let me be a good disciple of Christ to spread the gospel to all who can hear the good news that you sent your Son to die on the cross for the sins of all humanity, and whoever believes in Him shall not perish but have everlasting life.

Father, your Word tells me to be of strong courage and be not afraid. When I am anxious, you tell me to be still and know that you are on my side and shall not fear. You hold true to your word and to your promises.

During a crisis, you comfort me with the warmth of your love, grace, and mercy. You are always with me. Through you, I have the strength I need, and I walk my life in Christ with boldness and courage—you are my rock and my shield.

Father, you are all-powerful and all-knowing. You are the Most High who can do all things. Nothing is impossible to you. You know our hearts and our needs. Comfort those who need your healing power. Help those who cry out to you. Show blessings to all your children.

Father, I ask that you give faith to nonbelievers since you wish that no one should perish. Open their hearts to hear the truth of your Word and give them faith to believe. Teach me to love and pray for my enemies, and for those who persecute and hate me because of Jesus's namesake. Shield and protect me from the evil one. Thank you for my blessings. Forgive me of my sins. In Jesus's name. Amen.

The Word of God

"Every word of God is pure; He is a shield to those who put their trust in Him" (Proverbs 30:5).

Through the Blood of Jesus Christ

"In Him we have redemption through His blood, the forgiveness of sins, according to the riches of His grace" (Ephesians 1:7).

Be not Afraid

"Be strong and of good courage; do not be afraid, nor be dismayed, for the Lord your God is with you wherever you go" (Joshua 1:9).

Be Still

"Be still, and know that I am God" (Psalm 46:10).

Nothing is Impossible

"For with God nothing will be impossible" (Luke 1:37).

No One to Perish

"The Lord is not slack concerning His promise, as some count slackness, but is longsuffering toward us, not willing that any should perish but that all should come to repentance" (2 Peter 3:9).

Standing on the Promises of God

"Standing on the promises of Christ my King, through eternal ages let His praises ring, glory in the highest, I will shout and sing, standing on the promises of God ... Standing, standing, standing on the promises of God my savior, standing, standing, I'm standing on the promises of God" (Russel K. Carter, *Standing on the Promises*).

You may not hear this hymn in your church as often as it once was sung, but one thing is for sure, God stands by His promises. "Let us hold fast the confession of our hope without wavering, for He who promised is faithful" (Hebrews 10:23). Remember, His ways are not our ways, and neither is God's timetable on ours. God answers our prayers according to His will. We must ask God to give us faith and strength to do His will; then, God will bless us more than we can ever imagine. I pray for you that you allow God to be the pilot in your life. Let Him direct your steps to an abundant successful life in Christ. Reach out to Him today.

Prosperous and Successful Ways

"This Book of the Law shall not depart from your mouth, but you shall meditate in it day and night, that you may observe to do according to all that is written in it. For then you will make your way prosperous, and you will have good success" (Joshua 1:8).

Don't Worry

It is difficult to worry about your problems when you are praising and worshipping God. Let the peace of God reign in your heart and your worries will be washed away. Paul writes to the people of Philippi, "Be anxious for nothing, but in everything by prayer and supplication, with thanksgiving, let your requests be made known to God; and the peace of God, which surpasses all understanding, will guard your hearts and minds through Christ Jesus" (Philippians 4:6–7). Have you heard the saying, "Don't worry yourself to death"? Well, one can worry about something to the point of death.

Researchers at Yale University performed a study that showed a link between mental stress and death. It revealed that patients without heart disease had irregular rhythms and increased heart rates under stressful situations. Patients under mental stress with a pre-disposed heart condition may be more susceptible to sudden death[1].

Problems are going to happen. What you do about them is your choice. You can worry yourself to death, or you can let go and let God handle them. When a situation arrives, do not focus or dwell over something that you have no control.

Now, if, however, you have fallen into depression for long periods, and it begins to affect your life. I highly recommend seeking professional medical counsel. Do not delay reaching out for help. Everyone on this planet has been depressed about something. One can be depressed because of losing a family member. Someone may be depressed from losing their job, or because they did not get the job they wanted. However, when you lose interest in social activities, if you sleep more or have difficulty sleeping or eat more or have a loss of appetite, these conditions may suggest a form of depression in need of professional counseling or even medication. If you are in this situation currently, I hope you read the following prayer:

DRAW NEAR

Dear, Heavenly Father, you are an awesome God who can do all things. I come to you asking for healing for the broken-hearted. You love all your children. It is your will that we may be full of joy and peace.

Break the stronghold in the ones who have fallen to the lowest point in their life. Pull them out of their sadness and despair. Draw near to their hearts. Lift their spirits and give them happy and joyous days. When they speak to you, Father, hear and answer their prayers. Show them your loving-kindness and tender mercies. Let their ears hear the joy of your salvation through Christ Jesus.

Thank you, Father, for the blessings you have shown to us. We ask in the name of Jesus. Amen!

Take it to God

In my experience, depression feeds on doing nothing. When you dwell on your problems and don't do anything to correct them, you're feeding your depression. Take your issues to someone more prominent than any problem you may have—take it to God.

Ask God to get you through this situation. Don't keep these negative feelings within you. Turn them over to God and let Him help. Besides, it's God's will for you to be happy. He has promised to always be by your side. Set your sight on God and magnify the promises of Him. God's greatest promise to us is His unwavering love The apostle Paul tells us, "And we know that all things work together for good to those who love God, to those who are the called according to His purpose" (Romans 8:28). No problem is too big for God. Focus on how great God is and wait and see how small your problems become—He can do all things.

Apple of My Eye

King David was the apple of God's eye. During our rebellious and stubborn moments, we are His central focus. We are the apple of God's eye. Similarly, during our wayward moments, we should keep our focus on God. Ironically, He Becomes the apple of our eye.

"How happy he is whose wrong-doing is forgiven, and whose sin is covered! How happy is the man whose sin the Lord does not hold against Him, and in whose spirit, there is nothing false. When I kept quiet about my sin, my bones wasted away from crying all day long. For day and night Your hand was heavy upon me. My strength was dried up as in the hot summer. I told my sin to You. I did not hide … my wrong-doing. I said, "I will tell my sins to the Lord." And You forgave the guilt of my sin" (Psalm 32:1–5 NLV).

David poured out His heart to God asking for forgiveness. This should be a reminder for us when we pray to God. For God to forgive us of our sins, we must ask for His forgiveness. Prayers without asking forgiveness are like our words reaching the sky only to fall back to the earth.

MY ROCK AND SALVATION

Heavenly Father, you are worthy to be praised. I give you all the honor, glory, and majesty. Your kingdom is forever and ever. You are my rock and salvation. You are my strength and defense; I shall not be moved. I humbly come to you with an open heart for your divine wisdom and guidance.

I search deep to know you and your ways. Lead my steps to walk with integrity in your righteous ways. Lead my actions free from pride and arrogance. Teach me your loving kindness. Renew my mind and lock your holy Word in the bank of my heart.

Father, you are the author of peace. You will keep me in perfect peace. Whatever state I am in, I will be content, because I put all my trust in you. I pick up my shield of faith grounded in the gospel of Jesus Christ. Nothing can separate the love you have for me.

Keep my thoughts pure and clean. Purge my heart from any unrighteousness. Teach me your gentle wisdom, which is full of mercy and good fruits. I offer my body as a living sacrifice to you, Father, so that I may be acceptable to you. It is no longer I who lives but Christ who lives in me. Thank you for your never-ending grace.

I claim your promises God that you will not forget those who fervently love you. You are always with me during the good and the bad times. You never let go of me. Thank you for your unconditional love.

Rain down your gracious blessings on my family and me. Show abundant blessings to those who reverently fear you. Spread your tender mercies and loving-kindness to all your children. Lift our spirits with the joy of our salvation through your precious Son, Jesus Christ, our Lord and savior, is coming soon to take us home.

Guard and comfort those who are not well; heal them with your almighty power. Empower your disciples of Christ to boldly spread the good news that Jesus Christ is the only way to heaven. All who confess with their mouth that Jesus Christ is their Lord will be saved.

Father, I praise your holy name in the morning; I praise your holy name all day long. I will meditate on your Word day and night. I will follow your instruction to walk in obedience to do your will in my life.

Lead me from temptation and deliver me from evil and wickedness. Guard and protect my heart with your unfailing love, grace, and mercy. Thank you, Father, for hearing my prayer. Forgive me of my sins. In Jesus's holy name, I pray. Amen.

You are Worthy

"You are worthy, O Lord, to receive glory and honor and power; For You created all things" (Revelation 4:11).

Your Kingdom is Forever

"Your throne, O God, is forever and ever" (Psalm 45:6).

I Shall Not Be Moved

"He only is my rock and my salvation; He is my defense; I shall not be greatly moved" (Psalm 62:2).

Blessed are Those

"Blessed are the undefiled in the way, who walk in the law of the Lord! Blessed are those who keep His testimonies, who seek Him with the whole heart! They also do no iniquity; They walk in His ways" (Psalm 119:1–3).

Renew Your Mind

"Do not be conformed to this world, but be transformed by the renewing of your mind, that you may prove what is that good and acceptable and perfect will of God" (Romans 12:2).

Author of Peace
"For God is not the author of confusion but of peace" (1 Corinthians 14:33).

Perfect Peace
"You will keep Him in perfect peace, whose mind is stayed on You" (Isaiah 26:3).

Christ Who lives in Me
"I have been crucified with Christ; it is no longer I who live, but Christ lives in me; and the life which I now live in the flesh I live by faith in the Son of God, who loved me and gave Himself for me" (Galatians 2:20).

Reverent Fear

"My covenant was with Him, one of life and peace, and I gave them to Him that he might fear Me;

So he feared Me and was reverent before My name" (Malachi 2:5).

Only through Jesus

"I am the way, the truth, and the life. No one comes to the Father except through me" (John. 14:6).

God has the Power
"You shall remember the Lord your God, for it is He who gives you power to get wealth" (Deuteronomy 8:18).

I Know the Lord
Three people were on a beach, a young man, a middle-aged man, and an older man. The subject came up about who had the most knowledge. The young man reached down to the sand on the beach, cupping his hands full of sand and said:

"This is how much I know."

The middle-aged man spread his arms wide, scooping up an armful of sand and replied,

"Well, this is how much I know."

The older man picked up one grain of sand and said:

"This is how much I know of all there is to know. But when I get to heaven, I'll be perfect like my Lord Jesus and know all things."

We think the more knowledge we have, the better off we will be. Not so, if you do not know the only way to get to heaven is through Jesus Christ. Jesus tells us, "I am the way, the truth, and the life. No one comes to the Father except through Me" (John 14:6). If a person works on a farm for a living but cannot read or write but knows the Lord Jesus as His savior, he is a genius compared to the foolish rich man who denies Him.

Boast about the Lord

"This is what the LORD says: "Let not the wise boast of their wisdom or the strong boast of their strength or the rich boast of their riches, but let the one who boasts boast about this: that they have the understanding to know me, that I am the LORD, who exercises kindness, justice, and righteousness on earth, for in these I delight," declares the LORD" (Jeremiah 9:23-24 NIV).

Prayer is a sincere, sensible, affectionate pouring out of the soul to God, through Christ, in the strength and assistance of the Spirit, for such things as God has promised—John Bunyan

CHAPTER 12
Spirit of Power

"For God has not given us a spirit of fear, but of power and of love and of a sound mind"—2 Timothy 1:7

ON SOLID ROCK

Dear, Father, you are the Almighty God. No one compares to you. You are a loving God; You are a gracious God. You are good all the time. I come to you today on bended knees with arms raised toward the heavens proclaiming your honor, glory, and power.

Father, you are the fire that flames in my heart that shall never be extinguished. You put the glow in my eye and the joy in my steps; I can do all things through you. I boldly stand at the throne of your grace. You are my rock and my fortress; I shall not be moved. On the solid rock, I stand.

I praise and worship your holy name and love you with my whole heart. When I am anxious, you tell me to wait. You renew my strength. When I am afraid, you remind me that you did not give me a spirit of fear, but a spirit of power, love, and a sound mind. You give me peace and tell me to think of things, which are true, honest, just, pure, lovely, and of good report.

My commitment to you, Father, is to be transformed by your holy Word. I seek to do what is right and acceptable, and to do your will. I put all my trust in you, and in all my ways, you direct my paths. Father, I am steadfast, unmovable, and always abounding to walk in obedience. Nothing can convince me otherwise of the great love you have for me. Thank you for your unconditional love.

By your glorious power, you have saved me from eternal darkness through your precious Son, Jesus Christ. I am forever grateful for the grace you have extended to me. Teach me to extend loving-kindness and tender mercies to those who have hate and wickedness in their hearts. Keep me far from judging but bring me closer to be more loving as you have shown to me. Clean my heart from any unrighteousness. Fill it with the multitude of your love, grace, and mercy.

Show your gracious mercies to those who passionately seek you with all their hearts, and how abundant your blessings are for those who love you. Show wellness to those who are sick. Heal their bodies with your marvelous healing wonders. Uplift the broken-hearted and comfort their hearts with your unwavering love. Open the heart of non-believers since you wish no one to perish but have everlasting life. Deliver me from evil and lead me from temptation. Lead and direct my steps through the Holy Spirit to walk in your ways. In Jesus's name, I pray, Amen.

The Heavens

"Your mercy, O Lord, is in the heavens; Your faithfulness reaches to the clouds" (Psalm 36:5).

Fire in My Heart

"But His word was in my heart like a burning fire shut up in my bones" (Jeremiah 20:9).

Think of These

"Whatever is true, whatever is noble, whatever is right, whatever is pure, whatever is lovely, whatever is admirable—if anything is excellent or praiseworthy—think about such things" (Philippians 4:8 NIV)

The Throne of Grace

"Let us therefore come boldly to the throne of grace, that we may obtain mercy and find grace to help in time of need" (Hebrews 4:16).

Renew Your Mind

"And do not be conformed to this world, but be transformed by the renewing of your mind, that you may prove what is that good and acceptable and perfect will of God" (Romans 12:2).

Acknowledge Him

"Trust in the Lord with all your heart, and lean not on your own understanding; In all your ways acknowledge Him, and He shall direct your paths" (Proverbs 3:5–6).

Spirit of Power

"For God has not given us a spirit of fear, but of power and of love and of a sound mind" (2 Timothy 1:7).

Do the Will of God

"Do not love the world or the things in the world. If anyone loves the world, the love of the Father is not in Him. For all that is in the world—the lust of the flesh, the lust of the eyes, and the pride of life—is not of the Father but is of the world. And the world is passing away, and the lust of it; but he who does the will of God abides forever" (1 John 2:15–17).

Come to Repentance

"The Lord is not slack concerning His promise, as some count slackness, but is longsuffering toward us, not willing that any should perish but that all should come to repentance" (2 Peter 3:9).

My Eye upon You

"I will instruct you and teach you in the way you should go; I will guide you with My eye" (Psalm 32:8).

PRAY FOR THIS WORLD

Heavenly Father, you and you alone are the only true living God. I praise, magnify, and honor you with all my heart, mind, and soul. Thank you for your Son, my savior, and my deliverer, Jesus Christ. He whom you sent as a sacrifice to die on the cross for my sins. I humble myself before you, Lord; I need you. I put all my trust in you.

Give me the strength to stand against the evil in this world and those who are against you. Protect my family and me from wickedness. You are all-powerful, who can do all things. Heal my heart. Uplift my spirit with your tender mercies and loving-kindness.

Father, I pray for this world that you would comfort those who are persecuted and killed in the name of Jesus. Restore the joy of our salvation to all who love you across the world. Through your Son, we have an inheritance waiting for us in your kingdom. Lord, give faith to those who do not know your Son. Give them faith to believe that you wish no one to perish but come to you in repentance. So that they may turn away from their sins and follow Jesus Christ.

Father, teach me how to follow your will. Lead and direct my steps through the Holy Spirit to walk in obedience to you and show blessings to my family and me. Forgive me of my sins. In Jesus's name, I pray, Amen.

TEST THE SPIRITS

Heavenly Father, you are a sovereign God; there is none like you. I praise and worship your holy name and love you wholeheartedly. I come to you today with arms raised toward the heavens seeking your divine guidance.

Write your holy Word on the tablet of my heart so that I may apply it to my life, walking in truthfulness and righteousness. Be the light that directs my steps seeking your will and divine purpose. Teach me to discern your will in my life. May my ears be open to hearing your voice, and my eyes open to see your good ways.

Father, your Word says the beginning of knowledge is to fear the Lord. I have a reverent fear of you, Lord. Teach me wisdom to know you more. Lead me to be a faithful disciple spreading the good news of the gospel of our Lord Jesus Christ. Let me be not deceived by false teachings. But let me test the spirits knowing that my walk with you is holy as you are holy.

Your Word says that you are always with me and will never forsake me. You hold faithful to your promises. Wherever I go, you are there with loving opened arms. You give me peace and joy. You calm my soul. There is not a day that goes by that I do not praise your holy name. Thank you, Lord, for your never-ending love, grace, and mercy.

Heal the sickness in my loved ones. Find the right job for my family and friends. Strengthen my faith to walk with you in obedience. Deliver me from straying into the temptation of this world and keep the evil one away from my family and me. May the peace of Christ reign in my heart. Whatever I do, I do it in the name of Jesus. Show blessings to me and forgive me of my sins. In Jesus's name, I pray. Amen.

I LIFT MY EYES TOWARD THE HEAVENS

Heavenly Father, I lift my eyes toward the heavens in awe and acknowledge your marvelous creation, the earth, and all the things in the Universe. Marvelous are your mighty works and wonders. All your ways are trustworthy, steadfast forever and ever in faithfulness and righteousness. There is none like you. I love and serve you wholeheartedly and praise your holy name all day long.

Father, you hear and answer my prayer as it serves your will. Teach me how to distinguish between your will from my own. Open my ears to hear your voice when you answer me. I live my life in Christ grounded with unwavering faith, walking in obedience dependent upon you. I need you. I can do nothing without you.

In Jesus's holy name, purge my heart from any unrighteousness and cleanse me from my transgressions. Rain down your precious grace from heaven and wash away my sins, cleaning me white as snow. Keep me from doing what I do not want to do and lead me to do the things that I do not do. Forgive me, Father. Teach me to walk in the way of righteousness.

Father, I put you first above all things. I need more of you and less of me in my life. I put all my trust in you. You have placed me in a broad place and put love into my heart. Let your light direct my path and instruct my daily steps through the Holy Spirit to walk steadfast in the spirit. Free me from worldly things and surround me with holy ways.

Please help me be more mindful of others. Let the words of my mouth speak of love, joy, and peace. Let me praise your holiness in truthfulness and righteousness. Let me be an example of love and grace unto others as you have shown love and grace to me. Teach me to forgive others as you have forgiven me. Let my countenance in Christ shine that people see your good works in me.

I am forever grateful for the many blessings you have given to me. Most importantly, the grace you gave to this world by sending your precious Son, Jesus Christ, to die on the cross for the sins of humanity.

I pray for the Christians who are persecuted all around the world for Jesus's namesake. Let us hold fast to our confession that our Lord and savior, our king, is coming soon. Promote wellness to the sick. Heal them with your mighty hands. Strengthen marriages that have slipped away. Tug at the hearts of the unfaithful. Bring them to repentance and secure the loving bond you created. Comfort the broken-hearted with your tender mercies and loving-kindness. Lead those who are undertaking new journeys. Give them confidence and guide their decisions according to your will. Father, I ask that you open the hearts of unbelievers because you wish that no one perish but for all to have everlasting life.

Send financial blessings to my family and me and shower us with the abundance of blessings from your generous heart. Restore good health to us, Lord. Comfort us during trying times, and may your presence always be with us. Thank you, Father, for the unconditional love you have for me.

Father, you are worthy of all praise, honor, and glory. Your kingdom is forever. I lift my arms towards the heavens praising your holy name. Lead me from temptation and deliver me from evil. Let the peace of Christ reign in my heart in all that I do. In the name of Jesus, I pray. Amen.

The Way

If you are on the road of despair, the highway of corruption, or the path of deception—you are lost. God says, "Stand in the ways and see, and ask for the old paths, where the good way is, and walk in it; then you will find rest for your souls "(Jeremiah 6:16). If you say you cannot find God anywhere, ask God to find you—He will. "For the Son of man has come to save that which was lost" (Matthew 18:11).

Charles H. Spurgeon writes in His book, *All of Grace*: "The law is for the self-righteous, to humble their pride. The gospel is for the lost, to remove their despair. If you are not lost, what do you want with a savior? Should the shepherd go after the sheep that never went astray? Why should a woman sweep her house for pieces of money that were never out of her purse? ... If you are undeserving, ill-deserving, hell-deserving, you are the sort of person for whom the gospel is ordained and arranged and proclaimed. God justifies the ungodly" (Charles H. Spurgeon, pg. 20).

The Easy Way or the Hard Way

We all have heard this saying: you can learn things the easy way or the hard way. Of course, we will choose the easy way. We all want to be master planners. We want to orchestrate things the way we want them to go and not have someone else interfere with our plans. That would be learning the hard way. When we choose our plan and not God's plan, we are setting up ourselves for failure. If we choose God's way and follow His plan, then we choose the correct way.

The Way of Life

A young rabbit was walking down the trail in a forest. As he was entering unknown territory far from where his family had ventured, he was shivering in fear with every step. Still, he kept advancing further into the dark forest.

"Who goes there?" growled the bear of the forest.

The rabbit quivered, "It's me."

"Me who? I don't know of a me," said the bear.

"I am a forest rabbit who is seeking the way of life. I seem to be lost, sir, and was hoping you could direct me the right way."

"The little rabbit is lost and wants the bear of the forest to give him directions to the way of life," repeated the bear.

"Yes, please sir, show me the way of life. That's where I'm headed," the rabbit said.

The bear replied, "Many who travel down this route ask for the way of life. To the left, many travel because the path is wide, filled with green pastures and a life with no rules. However, it also leads to an ultimate death. To the right, is a narrow path that is difficult and filled with hardship and sorrow. Not many choose this path but it ultimately leads to life."

Forest

The confused rabbit said, "Why would I choose to die? If I go down the wide path, I am dead for sure. If I go down the narrow path, which is difficult, I don't know if I can make it on my own."

"Ah, your philosophy is backwards, little rabbit. The wide path is without guidance or instruction; you are on your own. The narrow path is filled guidance and instruction; you'll never be alone. The Spirit of the narrow path will lead you even during the difficult times so that you will always be protected. You may fall in a hole, but it will help you get out of it."

"I'm still confused," said the rabbit. "Why would anyone choose to go down a path that eventually leads to death? That doesn't make sense."

"The world deceives one into thinking it's better to see than to believe. There are many who are deceived. The narrow path is led by faith, which leads to life. The wide path is broad, and many follow it do not return," said the bear of the forest.

"There are those who return and did not die," said the inquisitive little rabbit?

The bear of the forest smiled, "Yes, there are those who chose the wide path first but eventually realized their choice was wrong and went down the narrow path."

"Well, I don't want to make that mistake. I'm choosing the right path; I'm seeking the way of life. From what you have advised me, I'm choosing the narrow path. Thank you, sir."

THROUGH THE BLOOD OF THE LAMB

Heavenly Father, I come to you today with a humble and open heart seeking your divine wisdom and instruction. You are the Almighty God who can do all things. You are worthy of all praise, honor, and glory. Your kingdom endures forever and ever. I praise and worship your holy name and love you with my whole heart.

Through the blood of the lamb, your Son, Jesus Christ, I have been made righteous with you. Your grace falls on me like a sweet rain from heaven, washing my sins white as snow. Thank you, Father, for your unconditional love, grace, and mercy you have for me. Lead and direct my steps and actions through the Holy Spirit to walk in obedience to your ways. So that I follow your will that you have planned for me. Lock your holy Word into the vault of my heart and surround it with truthfulness and righteousness.

Your Word says that your sheep hear your voice. You are my Shepherd. You lead me beside the still waters and restore my soul. During my troubles, you weather my storm and keep from worry. You protect me under the shadow of your wings. During my difficult times, you remind me that you are always with me and that you will not forsake me. Take my anger and frustrations and replace them with your love, joy, and peace. I may fail you Father, but you never let me down. Forgive me of any transgressions against you. Purge and clean my heart and wipe away any unrighteousness. You uphold me with your righteous right hand.

Your promises are true. When I cry out to you—you are already there. When I run to you, you accept me with arms wide open and embrace me with the warmth of your unfailing love. Through your holy Word, I fight the fight against any evil force that comes my way. I have no fear of anything or anyone but a reverent fear of you. You are my rock and shield. You are unchangeable, unmovable, and undefeatable. Nothing shall come between nor separate the love you have for me.

Father, I ask that you send financial blessings to my family and me. Shower your gracious blessings on to all those who seek and love you wholeheartedly. Heal those who are sick. Show your mighty healing wonders and restore health to them. Give faith to those who do not believe in your Son you because wish no one to perish but to have everlasting life.

Father, there is none greater than you. You are worthy of being praised. I praise you in the morning. I praise your holy name all day long. Guard and comfort my heart through the peace of Christ. Deliver me from temptation and evil and wickedness. In Jesus's holy name, I pray. Amen.

White as Snow

"Come now, and let us reason together," says the Lord, "Though your sins are like scarlet, they shall be white as snow; Though they are red like crimson, they shall be as wool" (Isaiah 1:18).

My Sheep Hear My Voice

"My sheep hear My voice, and I know them, and they follow Me" (John 10:27).

The Lord is My Shepherd

"The Lord is my Shepherd; I shall not want. He makes me to lie down in green pastures; He leads me beside the still waters. He restores my soul. (Psalm 23:1–3).

Shadow of Your Wings

"Be merciful to me, O God, be merciful to me! For my soul trusts in You; and in the shadow of Your wings I will make my refuge" (Psalm 57:1).

Righteous Right Hand

"Fear not, for I am with you; be not dismayed, for I am your God. I will strengthen you, yes, I will help you, I will uphold you with My righteous right hand" (Isaiah 41:10).

When I Cry to You

"Hear the voice of my supplications when I cry to You, when I lift up my hands toward Your holy sanctuary" (Psalm 28:2).

Ask in My Name

"And whatever you ask in My name, that I will do, that the Father may be glorified in the Son" (John 14:13).

Worthy to be Praised

"I will call upon the Lord, who is worthy to be praised" (Psalm 18:3).

The Narrow Road

Jesus told us in Matthew 7:13-14, "Enter by the narrow gate; for wide is the gate and broad is the way that leads to destruction, and there are many who go in by it. Because narrow is the gate and difficult is the way which leads to life, and there are few who find it".

Jesus says the narrow path is the way to eternal life, but it is a difficult path that will take us through hardships. Even though we may go through the dark valleys of life, Jesus is the Good Shepherd who will get us through them. The wide path, which leads to death and destruction, is easy. As you can witness in today's world, there are many who have chosen it. What must we do to get on the narrow path?

Jesus told us that *He is the way, the truth, and the life.* No one comes to the Father but through Him (John 14:6). We must deny ourselves, pick up His cross, and follow Jesus Christ with faith and obedience. We should be walking with the light of Christ even during trials and tribulations. We should be living our lives separately from the false pretenses of the world. Remember, the world tells you that you do not need God—you do!

If you adjust your life according to your plan, it will not work. If your plan is not working, it's because it's not *your* plan. God has a plan for me, and He has a plan for you. Let God work the plan He has designed for you. By doing so, you will understand what your plan is. We understand this through faith, trust, and by obeying God.

Narrow Flower Path

Tug of War

God has a plan for all of us. We all have different plans created by Him. When we ignore what He designed for us, we are going in the wrong direction. My testimony is that I went to church on Sunday but fell short the rest of the week. I was not seeking God every day. I was shaking hands with the good Lord on Sunday but dancing with the devil Monday through Saturday. I might as well have been considering I was not reading my Bible and talking to God daily. I was in a *tug of war* with myself. A great lesson to learn from this is you cannot pull from both ends and expect a great outcome. Whichever end you feed the most wins.

The anguish of many sleepless nights and hopeless days may drive one into a cave of misery. How you respond from being on the road of failure will pave a new road to success. The only way to get out of misery is only to serve one master. It's a choice. Here is what we should say:

"Lord, I have made many mistakes, I am not perfect, please forgive me of my sins. I believe Jesus Christ died for me, and I accept Him into my heart—In Jesus's name—Amen."

We may find it to be strange that God uses our hardships to get our attention. There's a moment when our life is in turmoil. When we are hanging on to a mere piece of thread falling to our knees. That's when we should say, "Lord, I cannot do this anymore. I need your help". Once we do this, we find true peace.

See the Light

It may be a difficult journey to reach that point when we lose ourselves, our identity, the people we are. We have trained and molded ourselves for protection from the harms of this world. Yet, Jesus asks of us to lose ourselves and come to Him. I was reluctant to give up being the person I worked so hard to become. Nonetheless, I really didn't like that person until the day I picked up my cross and followed Jesus. And from that moment until now, I haven't looked back. I *finally* saw the light at the end of the tunnel.

When we reach that place in our mind, out of its idle state, out of the land of confusion, and let loose the slippery rope of false hope, it is that moment when we can admit to ourselves about our sins or disappointments. It is when we become honest with ourselves and when it reveals who we are. It is the moment when we put to death the older person that we once were and become the person we were meant to be. Our vision becomes clear and focuses on God. We live every day carrying the cross of our Lord and savior, Jesus Christ. Paul tells us his story of that moment: "I have been crucified with Christ; it is no longer I who live, but Christ lives in me; and the life which I now live in the flesh I live by faith in the Son of God, who loved me and gave Himself for me" (Galatians 2:20).

My friends, if you have not made that step toward Jesus Christ, come to Him today. The Bible says, "That if you confess with your mouth the Lord Jesus and believe in your heart that God has raised Him from the dead, you will be saved" (Romans 10:9). Say this prayer:

"Lord, I accept you into my heart. I am a sinner. I need you in my life. Please forgive me of my sins. In Jesus's name, I pray. Amen."

Now is the time to find a church home if you have not already done so, but I recommend that you choose wisely. Find a church that teaches the Word of God and the gospel of Jesus Christ. Once you have decided, become its member. As a member of the church, after you have committed your life over to Jesus, you should be baptized in the name of the Father, the Son, and the Holy Spirit.

After baptism, you are born again; You are in God's royal family and a Christ-follower. Seek out God and listen intently to His instructions. When you follow God's plan, things will work out in your favor. God is never too late or too early; His timing is perfect. He is good all the time. Love the Lord with all your heart, mind, and soul. Love your neighbor as yourself. Be kind to one another, and love and pray for your enemies. Be an obedient and faithful servant to our Lord and savior, Jesus Christ and give thanks to our God Almighty for His abundant love, grace, and mercy. Let the peace of God always dwell in your hearts. Walk in the Spirit and live with love. God bless.

BIBLIOGRAPHY

Chapter 1
1   "Walking through doorways causes forgetting, new research shows". (n.d.). November 16, 2011. Retrieved from https://www.news.nd.edu/news/walking-through-doorways-causes-forgetting-new-research-shows.

Chapter 3
1   "How long does it take to form a habit". (n.d.), August 4, 200. Retrieved from https://www.ucl.ac.uk/news/2009/aug/how-long-does-it-take-to-form-a-habit.
2   Barry, M. S. December 2011. *The Forgiveness Project. The Startling Discovery of How to Overcome Cancer, Find Health, and Achieve Peace.* Grand Rapids, MI. Kregel Publications.

Chapter 4
1   Y J Draiman, January 14, 2011, "Little girl and her father were crossing a bridge". (n.d.) Retrieved from https://www.opednews.com/articles/Little-girl-and-her-father.

Chapter 8
1   Lyle, D. 1999. "Countdown to Apocalypse". Belfast: Ambassador Books. Pg. 21.

Chapter 10
1   Covey, S. 1989. "*The 7 Habits of Highly Effective People*". New York: Simon and Schuster.

Chapter 11
1   Jane Schwanke, "Yet Another Reason to Avoid Stress: Sudden Death", January 17, 2000. Retrieved from https://www.webmd.com/balance/stress-management.

ABOUT THE AUTHOR

Author, Darren Pettis RRT, is married to Becky. They have three daughters: Caitlin, Lindsey, and Cameron, and three grandchildren: Kennedy, Harrison, and Lennox. Darren received his Respiratory Therapy degree at Middle Georgia State University and studied Communication at Mercer University in Macon, Georgia.